C000182000

Consid___ _____

Christians and Creation

Care

2016

James Hindson

GILEAD
B O O K S
PUBLISHING

Gilead Books Publishing
Corner Farm
West Knapton
Malton
North Yorkshire YO17 8JB UK
www.GileadBooksPublishing.com

First published in Great Britain, August 2016

2 4 6 8 10 9 7 5 3 1

British Library Cataloguing-in-Publication Data:
A catalogue record for this book is available from the British
Library.

ISBN: 978-0-9932090-5-5

The publisher makes every effort to ensure that the papers used
in our books are made from trees that have been legally sourced
from well-managed and credibly certified forests by using a
printer awarded FSC & PEFC chain of custody certification.

Cover design: Nathan Ward
Cover image: Copyright © Michalakis Ppalis | Dreamstime.com

Contents

Preface

Recently I had a fascinating discussion about Christians and the environment with my son Tom. He is not yet a Christian but is always happy to discuss my faith and his beliefs. I should point out that Tom is a Politics and Philosophy graduate with a keen mind and, having been to Church regularly up to the age of sixteen, knows his Bible relatively well.

The first idea he proposed was that Christians are living lives of what he called "delusional necessity". He claimed that Christians have convinced themselves that all the creation-damaging activities we do each day without an apparent care for God's handiwork are necessary and hence acceptable. According to Tom, we have been deceived in the same way as the rest of the population. We think that our low cost flights, overheated homes, cheap food, two cars and all the other trappings of a twenty first century consumer society are *necessary* for a fulfilled Christian life. We have deluded ourselves into thinking that God wants us to live this way.

The second idea focused on how Christians treat the environment compared with other aspects of Christian living. In the case of most moral and social issues,

Christians look at what God's Word has to say and then follow his commands. It isn't easy at times but we generally don't ask for evidence that say, adultery, stealing, poverty, or many other issues have a negative effect on society before deciding whether to obey God or not. Clearly that would be totally ridiculous. God gives clear instructions that these things are wrong and hence He expects Christians not to do them! So why, Tom wondered, is it different when it comes to the environment? God tells us in Genesis that we should care for creation, so why do many Christians want evidence that our modern lives are harming the earth before obeying him? Why do so many Christians make excuses for creation-damaging behaviour? Surely that way of thinking is completely the wrong way round.

I believe that these two points, although difficult to accept, are worth careful consideration. Though perhaps harsh, they do seem to capture some of the key issues that I believe Christians need to understand before creation care becomes a normal pattern of behaviour in the same way as others are, such as not stealing, being kind to our neighbours, being truthful and not committing sexual sins.

These days it is difficult to escape from thinking about the effect our lifestyles have on the environment.

Evidence of thinking about the environment is all around us in the media, with words and phrases such as sustainable development, climate change and carbon footprints now part of our daily vocabulary and new ones appearing regularly such as 'low carbon economy' and 'green jobs'. Issues such as wind turbines, planning new transport routes, where our food comes from and the impact of cheap clothes from China are often in the news and we are frequently being asked to consider the environmental impact of our consumerism. The purpose of this book is to help understand where Christian thinking and action fit into this relatively recent focus on care for the environment. It is a short guide about how Christians should think about God's creation, how we should live in that creation and how we can escape from our consumerist creation damaging lifestyles.

The environment has been sadly neglected by Christians yet it is an area where Christians should be at the forefront of thinking and action. It's an area of Christian thinking and responsibility where we often let others do the leading, despite the fact that it is only Christians who have the real answers to the challenges of environment and sustainability. Our belief in a

Creator God carries with it huge responsibilities towards his creation.

Hopefully this book will provide a stimulating and readable encouragement to those Christians who perhaps are unsure that actively caring for God's creation is not optional but a requirement to be enjoyed as part of being a Christian disciple. It is also a book aimed at those who are already committed to a more positive environmental behaviour but need support to work out a distinctly Christian approach.

It is a purposely short book, intended to be simple but without avoiding complexity and thoughtful discourse where needed. It is divided into five sections. One way through the book is to start at the beginning and read to the end but there are other ways to the approach the different sections. If you want to start by knowing what the Bible says about creation care, then begin with Section Three, but if you are more concerned with specific practical action you can take then go straight to Sections Four and Five. Sections One and Two describe the current ecological mess we are in and how we got there.

This book is thoroughly rooted in the Bible as the inspired and infallible word of God and, assumes that in his Word, God has given us the principles he wants his people to follow in caring for his creation. The aim is to support, encourage and enable Christians who want to know more about their relationship to creation and how to behave in creation as part of creation. It is intended to be a pragmatic mixture of the theology of "creation care", the facts behind key ecological issues, the philosophical and the practical.

James Hindson

Shrewsbury
August 2016

Acknowledgements

This book has taken some time to write so huge thanks go to my wife Sue for her patience and support over these last few years. Others need thanking as well!

Thanks to my son Tom for allowing himself to be quoted in the introduction.

Paul Yeulett, Pastor at Shrewsbury Evangelical Church was also helpful in the early stages of writing and so thanks to him for the theological questions he posed about early drafts.

A really big thank you also goes to Peter Russell from Shrewsbury Baptist Church who read the final draft and offered many helpful comments from the perspective of an "ordinary Christian" as he calls himself.

Alice Matthews who as an English Language graduate and editor made many useful grammatical comments, tidying up my somewhat unpredictable style of writing.

Linsday and Anne Brown for reading an early draft and introducing me to a wide range of Christian thinkers on environmental issues through the Lausanne Movement.

Introduction

By background I am not a theologian but an environmentalist having spent most of my working life with an environmental education charity. Writing about the environmental content was relatively simple but I had to work harder on the theology - many thanks to those who helped with this. This is also the first Christian book I have written and in doing so I imagine that I share the same concerns as all Christian authors. I worry about hypocrisy in my own life in relation to the subject I am writing about. I am sure that no one who has written a book on prayer or Bible study, for example, would probably dare hold themselves up as a model to follow! And so it is with my ecological behaviour. I recognise the failings in my own life and know that I can do much better. For quite a time when working for an environmental organisation, to my great shame I failed to make the links between my work, my lifestyle and my faith. It was only when my work circumstances changed that I began to think much more clearly and was challenged in both my thinking and behaviour. Why it took me so long to take God's Word seriously in this area of my life I don't know, but at least I have now made start. I have a long way to go and there are many Christians who live much better creation care lives than I do. However, with God's help and guidance I pray that that my lifestyle is becoming closer to the lifestyle that honours him.

If reading this book clarifies thinking and action for you in the same way that writing it did for me then it will have achieved its goal. My prayer is that all Christians could be more enlightened about our relationship with the whole of God's creation and more equipped and encouraged to lead lives aligned with God's Word.

There is a lot of information about God's creation in this book. Sometimes the source of this information is referenced in the text but I have tried to avoid breaking up the flow of the writing too much. There is a short bibliography which lists the key publications and web sites where information can be found. I have made every effort to be honest in the way that information has been used and have only used trustworthy sources.

It is also worth saying that books like this one need to be read critically. Creation care is still a relatively new topic and, as a result, Christians are still struggling to understand exactly what God's Word says. It is highly likely that I have got things wrong from time to time for which I ask your forgiveness in advance. I would welcome a healthy and robust theological debate about

Christians and creation care. Please challenge my thinking with your own!

Chapter 1

How are we messing up creation and why?

1. What impact are we having on the earth?

When God finished his creation he looked at it and said that it was, "very good" (Genesis 1:21). His newly created world was perfect. As he considers his creation today does he still think the same? Is it still "very good?" Although God's creation is a wonderful place to be, the answer to the question is a firm "no". It is certainly not as good as he made it

People have an impact on the earth in two ways. We consume resources and we dispose of waste. Putting it in ecological language we use the earth as both a 'source' of things to support life and as a 'sink' for our waste. Of course it is more complex than this in reality, but most of the damage we do to the earth is a result of our greedy overconsumption of God's resources and the waste we produce as a result.

Most people are aware of the negative effects this overconsumption and waste has on ecological systems from local through to global levels. It would be possible to fill this book with examples of rivers that have been polluted by sewage killing most of the fish, wells that are running dry so people have no fresh water, oil spills that are almost impossible to clean up, air that is dangerous to breathe because of industrial gases, farm land that is losing fertility as a result of over use of pesticide and so on. Some of this damage can be repaired but often the results will be with the earth and its inhabitants for generations to come.

As well as individual examples, it is also possible to look at the ecological situation more systematically. The respected Stockholm Environment Institute (SEI) has identified nine 'planetary life support systems' at a global level and has noted that we pushing up to the boundaries of sustainability for each of these systems[1]. Their research suggests that in terms of the loss of biodiversity, climate change and soil depletion, we are way past the limits. We are heading for a situation where 30% of species God created could be lost by 2050 and we have already reached a situation where 70% of global fish stocks have gone, affecting not just diversity but food supply. We know that global patterns of climate are changing and if we carry on with 'business as usual' then we are looking at a rise in temperatures of at least four degrees Celsius by 2050, along with all that this will mean in terms of knock on effects. The thin layer of soil that God gave us to grow our food supply is also under huge stress in both developed and developing countries. The amount of nitrogen in the soil is in a critical condition and huge amounts of fertile soil are lost through erosion. Then there are other issues related to water supply, with the number of people experiencing water stress increasing, especially in Africa and parts of Asia. Other systems such as the acidification of the oceans are still within what the SEI considers to be a safe limit, but these too are accelerating towards the danger limits more quickly year by year.

This information should dismay as we realise that many of the things that God has freely provided have nearly been used up and that much of the waste we produce is so toxic that people and animals are dying as a result. Every day the media is filled with ecological horror stories that often leave people astounded that we can cause so much damage. However worrying as these examples of human damage to creation are, as individual events they don't illustrate an overall impression about the health of the earth. Looking at individual disasters is rather than the whole picture is a little like the difference between a doctor looking at one part of your body that hurts or giving a general health check. Just as healing some specific pain can give the impression that all is well with our body as whole, successfully cleaning up one localised mess can encourage us to think that all is well with the earth as a whole. That is where we are deluded. A better way of understanding the seriousness of the situation would be to use a single measure that clearly demonstrates the severity of the overall global challenge.

One of the most powerful indicators of global unsustainability is a wonderful metaphor for the impact we are having on the earth - the 'ecological footprint'[2]. Who has not taken great pleasure in running across a newly washed beach then looking back and seeing the trail of footprints or writing their name on the immaculate sand? For some reason it gives us perhaps a childish thrill that we have made our mark on the beach. The ecological footprint is a measure of the impression that our lifestyles leave on the earth. It is calculated by working out the amount of land needed to provide all the things we consume (such as food, clothing and other things we buy) added to the amount of land needed to take all our waste. It is usually expressed as the number of hectares of land needed by a single person each year to support the lifestyle they have chosen. Thinking of it in terms of human health, the size of someone's ecological footprint is a little bit like the blood pressure of a particular lifestyle. It is a measure of how healthy that way of living is.

It has been calculated that if everyone on the earth had a **theoretical** equal share of the resources God has provided then their ecological footprint would be around 1.8 hectares per person. This would be a sustainable footprint. The **actual** size of the average global footprint however is around 2.2 hectares per person. This means that on a global scale, each year we are consuming more resources than we have available. It doesn't take much common sense to realise that this cannot be a good idea and certainly cannot carry on forever.

Not only is it the case that globally we are consuming more than we have but the size of the ecological footprint is very different in different countries. The ecological footprints for a selection of countries is shown in the table below and the figures highlight a number of disturbing facts about the tremendously unsustainable way in which we are using God's earth[3].

Country	Footprint in 2007 (hectares)
Indonesia	1.21
India	0.91
Kenya	1.11
Thailand	2.37
China	2.21
Brazil	2.91
South Africa	2.32
Poland	4.35
Germany	5.08
Japan	4.73
Italy	4.99
United Kingdom	4.89
USA	8.00

The figures show that the average footprint of a person in the more developed and richer countries of the world is between 5 and 10 hectares per person. A typical person in the UK has a footprint of just over 5 hectares and people in the United States, 8 hectares. At the other end of the scale people in most African and Asian countries have footprints of around just 1 or 2 hectares. Remember, these figures indicate how much land is needed to support our lifestyles and the rather bland numbers tell us that the lifestyles of those in richer countries mean that we consume and waste far more than our fair share, whilst many people have much less than their fair share. Putting it another way, if everyone on the earth had the same size footprint as we have in the UK then we would need the resources of just under three earths to provide all the resources to support that lifestyle. God has very generously given us one very productive earth and that should be enough to sustain ourselves! To make matters worse, the footprint of people in most countries is actually growing year by year. In 1960 the United Kingdom footprint was 3.9 hectares, Germany's 3 hectares and Japan's just 2.

You might be asking, how is it possible to use 4.6 or 10 hectares per person when only 1.8 hectares are available? How can some countries use three times their fair share? Where do these 'extra' resources come from? Think of it this way. If you are lucky enough to have significant savings in the bank you might try and live on the interest from that investment leaving the capital safe in the bank. That's what the 1.8 hectares per person represents, the interest on the 'natural' or 'ecological' capital that God has provided. Natural capital that God has ensured regenerates itself from year to year. The fact that we are using more than the 1.8 hectares tells us bluntly that each year we are eating a little bit more into this capital. It doesn't take a mathematical genius to work out that this cannot carry on forever. The table below shows how serious the situation is in some countries. An ecological surplus means that the country has more natural capital per person than is consumed, and a negative figure shows when the people in country are consuming more than they have. Each year, every person in the UK consume 3.5 hectares of resources more than the country can supply. The governments of many countries are worried about financial deficits. They should be just as concerned, if not more so, by ecological deficits.

Country	Ecological surplus (+) or deficit (-)
Indonesia	+0.14
India	- 0.40
Kenya	- 0.52
Thailand	- 1.22
China	- 1.23
Brazil	+6.07
South Africa	-1.28
Poland	-2.26
Germany	-3.16
Japan	-4.13
Italy	-3.85
United Kingdom	-3.55
USA	-4.13

The information on the table[4] also highlights another issue to do with ecological justice. How can it be that people in the richer western countries can consume so much, yet run an ecological deficit? The answer is simple. They are not actually eating into their own natural capital because that was used up long ago. What these rich countries are doing is buying their natural capital from other countries and from future generations. They are then using the capital they have purchased to protect and maintain their current unsustainable lifestyles. It should bring tears to our eyes to realise that despite living in the twenty first century, at least one third of the world's population do not have access to the most basic of God's free gifts of sufficient food, energy and water, and that is partly because those in the richer countries are consuming much more than their fair share.

The essential message is therefore that, contrary to what we sometimes choose to believe, our consumption in global terms is seriously unsustainable. Although as individuals we might think we live simple lifestyles, we need to realise that everything is relative. What might appear simple living, to us, to someone in an Indian village for example, is incredibly complex. In our connected and interdependent world, it is important to realise that we cannot take the benefits of living in a globalised world and be deluded into thinking that we should not shoulder any of the responsibility. We just cannot continue for much longer consuming more than is available. We know that this kind of living doesn't work for an individual household and it won't work for the planet either.

2. The challenge of climate change

There is no doubt that the climate of the earth is changing for the worse and that humans are the major cause. Although some may dispute this, the evidence is overwhelming. The earth is wonderfully made. When God created the atmosphere he gave it a particular balance of gases that allowed humans, plants and animals to live. Scientists have called some of these gases 'greenhouse gases' because one of their functions is to help to keep the temperature of the earth just right for the life God created. Without this balance the average temperature of the earth would be a fairly cold minus 30 degrees Celsius! However, over the last two hundred years, human activity has changed the balance by adding vast quantities of greenhouse gases to the atmosphere, mainly carbon dioxide and methane. This has happened largely as a result of using fossil fuels such as coal, oil and gas alongside an increase in large scale agricultural practices. According to God's original plan this extra carbon dioxide should not be there and its impact has been to stop heat escaping from the earth into the atmosphere. This has caused the earths' temperature to rise. The science of how this happens is relatively complex but the fact is simple - the average temperature of the earth has risen by around one degree Celsius over the last 100 years[5].

The problem has been made worse by other unthinking human activity. To help keep the balance of gases right God created a number of 'carbon sinks' to absorb any excess greenhouse gases that might be produced. However, as well as putting too much carbon dioxide into the atmosphere, humans have also been reducing the capacity of these sinks to absorb greenhouse gases thus exacerbating the problem. The Amazon rainforest is a good example of a global carbon sink and the deforestation of tropical rainforests worldwide probably biggest damage being done by humans.

Then there are also "feedback effects" that make the problem even worse! For example, as the temperature of the earth rises then vast areas of previously permanently frozen ground in Siberia and northern Canada will begin to melt. As they do the methane that had been locked up in them for thousands of years will be released into the atmosphere causing further rises in temperature.

Of course the climate change story is far more complex than this but those are the basics. We're putting too much carbon dioxide and other gases into the atmosphere whilst at the same time reducing the capacity of God's creation to absorb these gases. And so the average temperature increases.

Before the start of the nineteenth century the proportion of carbon dioxide in the atmosphere was around 250 parts per million. This doesn't sound much but in 1800 it started to rise as a result of the coal burned to provide energy for the industrial revolution, and rose again the twentieth century when we added oil as a fuel. It now stands at just over 400 parts per million. By 2050, it will probably reach 450 parts per million, if not more. It is this increase in the proportion of carbon dioxide which has caused the average temperature of the earth to rise by around one degree Celsius over the last one hundred years. Because the most important greenhouse gases stay in the atmosphere a long time, even if we could stop producing them tomorrow the temperature would still rise by another two or three degrees by 2050. How much more it rises is largely up to us, but if our global economic behaviour continues along the path we are currently following then we could be looking at an increase of four, five, or even six degrees Celsius by 2100. The worrying fact is that scientists suggest that anything over a three degree rise might have potentially disastrous impacts on the way different ecological systems work, such as the ability of creation to provide the food we need.

Dramatic climate change has the potential to bring global catastrophe. Ecologists have always known that everything in creation is delicately linked together and that changes in one part of an ecosystem will cause ripples of change throughout the whole ecosystem. Natural systems are constantly adjusting to changing conditions. After a severe storm or forest fire, both of which destroy trees and wildlife, these ecosystems restore themselves naturally. It takes time but ecosystems are incredibly robust. Natural systems can also adapt if the temperature increases, but only if it happens very slowly and over a long time period. The problem is that what we are now experiencing is in an altogether different league. Scientists are beginning to record evidence of natural systems on a global scale being thrown out of balance by the slowly increasing global temperature. They also fear that the possibility of these natural systems being restored is slight.

The changes that are happening to the atmosphere on a global scale are difficult to measure and making predictions about the impact of the changes, even using robust and powerful computer models, can be an uncertain business. There are many unanswered questions in the global warming equation and sometimes the global trend of warming appears to go into reverse and we experience short term colder weather. It is also recognised that the climate of the earth has changed naturally. For example, Roman Britain was warmer than it is today. These changes are not disputed or challenged. However, it is important to stress two things. The first is that none of the uncertainties negate the basic fact that the earth is warming and this warming will have severe consequences unless it is radically checked. The second is that climate changes in the past were a result of God created natural cycles and not a result of human activity. Today things are different. It is humans causing the change.

3. What is going to happen in the future?

Temperature rise brings with it an associated range of local and global scale problems the impacts of which are already being felt, especially by poorer people in some of the world's poorer countries. In the medium and long term nearly everyone on earth will be affected both directly and indirectly. Climate change is serious.

Sometimes people, Christian included, make jokes about climate change. Whilst it is true that some of the countries of northern Europe will be warmer and perhaps have less snow in winter and warmer summers, overall there will be many more losers than winners. Here are just some of things that are predicted as a result of the increase in temperature we shall experience. Some are taking place right now, whilst others are likely to appear over the next ten years or so. It is a shocking list.

- Sea level is rising and will continue to rise as a result of melting ice and the thermal expansion of the oceans - as sea water warms up it expands. This rise in sea level is already causing more frequent floods in low lying coastal areas. A further sea level rise will result in a loss of valuable farm land and space for people to live in. Many coastal communities both large and small could be under threat.

- Increasing temperatures could make some parts of the earth so hot that it will be near impossible to live there. As a result, there could

28

be mass movement of people to cooler climates adding to the migrations caused by sea level rise.

- Melting glaciers and ice sheets will cause short term flooding. More seriously there will be a shortage of drinking water for the millions of people in China and India that rely on the annual ice melt for water supply. Drinking water in coastal areas will also be affected by sea level rise.

- Rising temperatures can cause changes in weather patterns leading to an increase in unpredictable floods, hurricanes and other extreme weather events such as heat waves and droughts.

- A reduction in food supply is likely because of the lower productivity of crops at higher temperatures and a change in the places in the world where crops can be grown.

- The rise in temperature is already changing habitats for plants and animals leading to the extinction of a number of species. The rate of these extinctions will increase.

- In some parts of the world there will be an increasing incidence of disease.

With good planning we shall be able to mitigate or adapt to many of these impacts such as sea level rise. Others are more serious, especially the possible impacts on food and water. But when are these impacts going to happen? How much time is there to come up with solutions?

This is a difficult question to answer because scientists have generally underestimated the speed at which climate change is having an impact on parts of the earth. Just one example will suffice. The speed at which the ice at both the north and south poles is melting is faster than predicted. This ice is globally important because the colder temperature of the Arctic is largely responsible for the pattern of ocean currents in the northern hemisphere and it is these currents that help to distribute heat around the earth, like swishing water around a bath! As this ice declines significantly currents might change and the impact of climate change becomes less predictable!

Nearly all leading politicians, economists and scientists now agree on the very real chance of a climate change disaster in the future. Although they differ on the detail there is agreement that there is a strong possibility that the life support systems that God created could be irreparably damaged. Of course there are some dissenting voices, but the disagreements are not so much about the facts, but about when it will happen, what should be done and who should pay for it. The resources we need to survive on Earth are running out, the sinks where we throw our waste are filling up and the earth will be a minimum of two degrees hotter by 2050, even if we stopped releasing any carbon dioxide into the atmosphere tomorrow. There are plenty of books about the future of the earth under different climate change conditions. Some describe in great detail what will happen if the temperature reaches up to six degrees more than it is now, which it could well do under some business-as-usual models. Others take lessons from history and describe civilisations in the past that have destroyed themselves through an over use of resources. The scientific and popular media use very different languages but both paint a similarly bleak picture.

Despite the efforts many countries are making the average temperature of the earth is still rising. It is true that there are thousands of examples in our lives where things are getting better. We are using more renewable energy, travelling more by bus, train and cycle, making efforts to be more energy efficient in our homes and work places, and recycling more. The list could go on. However, it is also true to say that few, if any global indicators of ecological quality are improving and the impacts of climate change and over use of resources are being felt at an ever increasing rate, especially in many developing countries. The current situation has been likened to walking north on a southbound train. You are trying to move in one direction but are going in the opposite one. Think of it in human terms; your dimming eyesight might now be much better as a result of an operation, but doesn't mean that overall you are any healthier! A whole person solution is needed. Similarly, a 'whole earth' solution is needed.

We don't have a huge amount of time to come up with the right answers with the pessimists saying that we have less than ten years to make a real change and the optimists giving us a maximum of fifty years. The difference between the optimists and pessimist is small in the big picture of things. Critical and radical decisions need to be made within our own life time.

Having got all that gloom and doom out of the way there are also some positive things to say. Although we shall have to accept living in a hotter world there is agreement that solutions exist right now to make sure that it doesn't rise higher than this. There are also solutions around to help us to adapt to the different world that climate change will bring. It will be tough and costly but through God's grace, the technologies needed to ensure that we can live a God honouring quality of life are already available. We also have the resources to raise the quality of life for people who currently experience economic and ecological poverty. Although the solutions are expensive, the sooner we bite the bullet and pay for them the more cost effective they will be. As the government commissioned report by Lord Stern in 2006 so clearly demonstrated, every year of delay results in a higher cost to bear in the future.

The problem is that as well as their cost, the solutions require a complete revolution in how our economy is structured and a complete change in how people behave. Nothing new for the Christian in those conclusions, but it is necessity of these huge changes that scare global decision makers. So whilst by and large we have the means to change, what we don't have is the political and social will to put them into practice.

4. Can we trust what we are being told?

Some of you might be saying, 'it can't be as bad as all that. Have the scientists and other experts really got it right?'

The short answer is 'yes' - and those Christians who doubt whether the earth is in an ecological mess are quite simply wrong! Of course, the scientists and other experts such as economists don't know everything there is to know about the earth's resource, population growth and climate. It is proper to intelligently question scientific evidence and the interpretation of some of the data. Scientists are sinners too. However, to ignore the evidence about the ecological challenges we are facing is about as sensible as questioning whether smoking tobacco causes cancer. There are very good reasons for believing the evidence presented to us about our impact on the earth.

There are thousands of scientists working in many different fields all coming to conclusions that tell a similar story. It is difficult to escape from the sheer weight of the evidence. For example, the regular reports from the Intergovernmental Body on Climate Change (IPCC, a United Nations organisation) take information from the scientists whose job it is to collect, collate and interpret the scientific data and

34

make conclusions based on this data. The IPCC, has a fair number of Christian scientists on it and is a fairly conservative body. It doesn't use tabloid style headlines and it has taken its time before coming to the conclusion that the observed rise in temperature of the earth was a long term trend and that this rise was caused by human activity. When a body like the IPCC warns against the impacts of climate change it deserves to be listened to. The evidence presented is robust, trustworthy and demands to be taken seriously.

Although it is possible that scientists might be wrong about some of the data, it is highly unlikely that they are all wrong about everything. It is true that history does have plenty of examples of scientists who bucked the scientific position of their day and were right, but none of those issues are really comparable with the current global situation we are facing. In most cases the challengers, such as Galileo and Copernicus, usually had evidence that demonstrating that the accepted orthodoxy was wrong and were soon proven right once some the pressures to conform were lifted. God has given us what we like to call 'common sense' as well as our intelligence and we have a responsibility to use them both. Whilst the impact of climate change or biodiversity loss is not yet being felt seriously in the western world it is happening. As has been suggested, we are protected from many of the effects of climate change by our wealth and, because we do not live as close to the natural world as we used to, we are isolated from the impact it is having.

Having said that, you may still be sceptical. Here are two other arguments: A previous chapter listed nine key planetary life support systems and the unsustainable ways in which we are using God's creation as a result of our over consumption and wasteful lifestyles. It might be possible to suggest that one or more of the systems has not been damaged to extent that is claimed, but there is hardly any informed person on earth, Christian or otherwise, who would suggest that none of them are being damaged. If even one is affected then surely that would be a bad thing and should cause us to question how we are caring for God's creation.

Even if evidence and logic don't persuade, there is always 'Pascal's Wager', the idea that it is safer to believe in something that *isn't* true than to not believe in something that *is* true. Even if you don't really believe that climate change is happening you might as well go along with it and take action to reduce your impact on the earth. Why? Because even if you are right and climate change is not happening then at least you are no worse off. If, on the other hand, you are wrong and it is happening then you will have made a contribution towards restoring God's creation, albeit reluctantly. If this helps persuade some that Christians should behave differently towards God's creation then I am happy enough to go along with it!

5. We are in this mess because we consume too much stuff

Of course, the ultimate cause for the mess we are in is our sin. Adam's first sin has affected creation for all time just as it affected the whole human race. It will carry on having an impact until we have a new heaven and a new earth. However, just to say that sin is the cause of something is never a very helpful answer when trying to help diagnose and then tackle a problem. Neither is it the answer that we give when considering other issues. We need to find out more to know how Christians can best work towards responding in a biblical way and in the case of our impact on God's earth there are two "big picture" ways in which sin has caused this mess.

Firstly, we consume too much stuff and secondly, this stuff is made in the wrong way.

The Devil has been extremely clever in deluding the whole human race, Christians included. Not content with damaging the human part of God's creation through tempting Adam and Eve, he has also been working with our own selfish sinful nature to provide a whole range of distractions that result in us damaging creation! Put simply, this sin is called "greed", and is a breaking of both the eighth and tenth commandments. It is what the writer of Ecclesiastes warned against in chapter four, and is precisely what Jesus was talking about in his conversation with the rich young ruler recorded in Luke chapter twelve! How has the Devil done this? How is our greed related to a lack of creation care? Are we really greedy in the way Jesus has defined greed? How does greed work?

The Devil has influenced us to define ourselves not by 'who we are' but by 'what we buy' - through our possessions, position and lifestyle. This is evident in the world around us and increasingly amongst Christians. It works like this: If we judge ourselves and others by what we have rather than who we are, then by definition we need to 'have' more and more. In this consumerist society, more and more is thought to mean better and better and, therefore, happier and happier! Every time a product is made to satisfy our hunger for ever more 'things' another part of God's creation is uprooted, dug up or killed to provide it. One author has neatly called this the "affluenza virus" which is perhaps a more acceptable phrase than the word sin, as it suggests that there is a human cure[6]. Whatever it is called, the virus of excessive consumption is spreading and causing ecological havoc in its wake.

Although Christians appear to be less affected by the virus than others it is also true to say that we all have this addiction to some extent. This delusion is so sad because Christians are a distinctive force for good in so many areas of society. Historically Christians have led the way on social issues such as the abolition of slavery, free education, and prison reform. Currently we campaign on the challenges of poverty, euthanasia, child slavery, the trafficking of women, as well as working with people in prison, those with financial challenges and addictions. Christians throughout the world are involved actively in social issues but one area in which we have failed God and where the Devil has so cunningly deluded our thinking is in our consumerism!

No doubt the Devil rubs his hands in glee each time our sinful natures lead us to go shopping as a recreational activity or when we buy a product for which we have no real use or when we buy a 'new something' to replace a perfectly good 'old something' we already have. The list could go on. Of course, we need some stuff to live a God honouring quality of life. The issue is whether the stuff we buy is necessary and how we have been persuaded or deluded ourselves into thinking it is 'necessary'. Perhaps this is an unfair judgement as there are some who have not been affected by this virus, but even those that have so far escaped maybe don't realise that this sin is one of the root causes of our current ecological crisis. Add up all the unnecessary stuff we have in our homes (and sometimes in our churches) and work out where the materials for them all came from and you may end up being shocked.

This excess consumption is not just damaging the ecology of the earth but it is also failing to satisfy the promises that lead us to consume. According to the story we are being sold, consumption is meant to make people happier. It's meant to help us define ourselves and to feel good about life! Why have Christians been deluded by this consumption fairy tale? We are constantly warned by God about relying on things for our security. The writer of Ecclesiastes tells us that 'all labour and achievement spring from man's envy of his neighbour. This too is meaningless!' (Ecclesiastes 4:4). In the Parable of the Sower it was the distractions of this world that led to failure of the seed falling on stony ground (Mark 4:17-18). If warnings from God's word are not enough, then perhaps research evidence might help. Scientifically based measures of perceived happiness show that despite people in the richer countries getting wealthier, personal happiness has not increased for the last forty years[7]. In many areas of life things have worsened due to increasing personal stress, emotional and mental breakdowns, failed marriages, and damaged children as everyone tries to keep up with the treadmill of consumption. It also has resulted in such an unequal distribution of God's resources on earth that it is both immoral and obscene.

The messages are clear. Greed and overconsumption is bad for your health, bad for the earth and bad for our relationship with God. The problem is that we have let the Devil delude us otherwise!

6. We are in this mess because we make things in the wrong way

When unthinking consumption is linked to the unthinking production then we have created a destructive force like no other. Not only are we are buying and consuming too much and judging ourselves and others by possessions, it is also the case that we produce the things we buy in really harmful ways. This is illustrated in the diagram below:

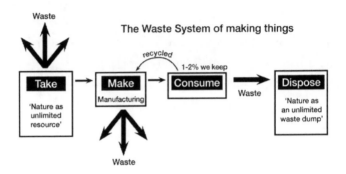

This diagram highlights the core of the problem. It shows a system which produces more waste than 'things'. Nearly every product we consume - clothes, electrical goods, furniture, the houses we live in, and even our food – is produced in this way. If you look at the life cycle of any product from the moment the raw materials are taken out of the ground through to the time it is disposed of, more waste is produced than product itself. You just have to think of the waste produced during the manufacture of a simple product like a cotton t-shirt. Firstly, there is the cotton for the shirt which was grown using around 1kg of pesticides and fertilisers. Growing enough cotton for making a t-shirt also uses 10,000 litres of water, often in countries ill able to afford water being used in this way.

The manufacturing process creates around 20kg of carbon dioxide for each t-shirt. Around 250 grams of dyes are used to make a coloured t-shirt, dyes that may well be toxic and disposed of in streams near the factory. Then there is all the waste produced in the transport process as the t-shirt is moved from a factory (say, in China) to your nearest high street. To add insult to injury, as a result of our 'affluenza' many people don't even need or possibly really want the t-shirt they buy in the first place. The average clothing spend in many richer countries is over £500 per person each year. On average we purchase one item a week and over the period of a year, each person sends 15 kilograms of clothes to landfill. '*But I give my old clothes to charity*,' I hear you say. Well, that's better than nothing, but it is kind of odd, isn't it? An underpaid worker goes to all the trouble in China to make you a t-shirt, trashing the earth along the way. You wear it once or twice and then it gets recycled – and maybe then sent back to China![8]

This process has been called the Take, Make and Waste system for obvious reasons. As a society we have become experts at spending vast amounts of money on making and buying goods that we simply bury or burn when we have finished with them. This system is even more horrifying when we take into account the human waste involved in making all the stuff we buy. It is still the case that the cotton for our t-shirts might have been harvested by children in Uzbekistan, and many t-shirts are made by people exploited in poorer countries. Often they are paid less than a living wage, have poor working conditions, and often very few or no employment rights.

If it is the case that this system is at the root cause of our current ecological mess, how did we let this happen? How did this rather crazy system come into being?

The system shown in the diagram only works because the people who make the things don't pay the true cost of the making them, and as a result the people who consume them don't pay the real price for them. This might sound odd, so let me explain. Consider your t-shirt again. The farmer grows the cotton and the t-shirt manufacturer buys it paying so much per kilo to cover the famer's costs (wages, fertiliser, pesticides, energy, machinery etc.). However, there is a long list of things that the t-shirt manufacturer does not pay for and that is not included in the price of cotton. Because the final consumer (you and me) wants a really cheap t-shirt, the farmer has to sell his cotton at a competitive price and so cuts costs as much as he can. For example, child labour is used on many cotton farms because children are cheaper to employ. The cost per kilo of cotton, and hence of your t-shirt, does not compensate the children for the loss of valuable school time. Neither might it cover the cost for extra health care needed because of the effect of pesticides. Nor would it cover the cost of the bottled water those who live near the farm have to buy because their wells have run dry as a result of the cotton farmer taking all the water. The number of things not included in the price of your low cost t-shirt increases when the cotton reaches the factory in some big Chinese city, when it is transported to your local high street and even in the chain store itself!

The list of problems caused by our demand for a cheap t-shirt could go on and on and take up a whole book. Economists call these issues externalities, and they are not included in the price we pay. Do we honestly think that one pound (the cost of a t-shirt recently in one low cost store) could ever possibly cover the true cost of making a t-shirt? Can one pound give all those involved in making your t-shirt a decent standard of living and environment to live in? Of course it doesn't, and we must be deluded if we think it does.

So who does pay? There are two possibilities, both of which are tragic. Either no one pays, meaning that the people and the environment suffer, or the bill for the ecological and human damage caused is picked up by a much poorer government than ours. It is this deliberate 'forgetfulness', greed and delusion that allow so much of the stuff that we buy to be so cheap. If we had to pay the true cost of things, then we would buy much less. Demand would be lower, fewer things would be produced and the earth and people would be whole lot better off! It really is time that Christians challenged our "throw away" society in a serious way.

Another factor which has allowed this wasteful system to flourish is that everyone has an expectation of continued economic growth. This is usually a personal aspiration, but it is also an expectation of society as a whole including the banking system and business. Because we have been infected and deluded by sin and greed, we have allowed ourselves to be persuaded by economists, business people and politicians - people that our economy must constantly grow to allow us as individuals to get wealthier, buy more stuff, increases our quality of life and get happier and happier! But just think about it for a moment; a constantly growing economy, whatever that really means, is almost guaranteed to result in ecological disaster. To continue earning more money year by year, somebody somewhere has to make more things and people have to buy them. And making this stuff has an impact on God's created world. This has to happen faster and faster each year because an economy that is growing by, say, just one per cent each year, is growing in exponentially. In other words, growth gets faster and faster each year. An expectation of constant economic growth will condemn the earth to ecological disaster sooner or later. We hope later – but as we have seen, no one really knows! In the end our greed will be our undoing.

So where did this desire for a constant increase in growth come from? That is a long story involving the history of the banking system, the rise of the corporation and attitudes to money and making money. We have been persuaded through a whole variety of subtle and sometimes not so subtle methods that our goal in life is personal happiness and success, and we have been persuaded that the main way in which these are measured is by the things we possess, rather than the quality of our lives or who we are. We believe we have to buy more stuff to achieve what we are told is happiness. The Devil manages this process quite cleverly through, amongst other things, the media. If we believe it and follow it, then more of God's creation has to be destroyed each year to make the things to sell to provide what we think we need for our ever increasing wealth and happiness! It is down to simple mathematics. Exponential growth like this on a finite earth is just not possible.

7. What about population growth?

Both Christians and non-Christians sometimes like to blame global population growth for the current ecological crisis. Although they don't often say it directly, it is often implied that countries with large and fast-growing populations are at fault. It needs to be said firmly that this is untrue.

It is a strange belief to hold. Most people living in richer countries would agree that the quality of life for many people in poorer countries needs be improved but conveniently seem to forget that any improvement usually means having more things. Even basic human rights such as access to clean water and sanitation and electricity in your home, things we take for granted, require stuff to be made. People in poorer countries also aspire to possess other things as well that we have access to without thinking, such as cars, washing machines, the internet, well equipped schools and hospitals and so on. Having these things also requires using natural resources. Thankfully, more and more people in the world are getting just that little bit richer and are able to buy these things. So why blame the ecological crisis on them achieving a slightly better standard of living rather than ourselves? That seems unfair.

Even with a slightly increased consumption, most people in countries with larger population growth rates have smaller ecological footprints per person than richer western countries with populations that are growing slowly or in some cases getting smaller. For example, a baby born in Europe today will have consumed around ten times as much of God's creation by the time he or she is five compared with a baby born in most parts of India.

This is not to say that the population capacity of God's earth is unlimited, or that the rate of population growth will cause more problems in the future. We cannot have a continually increasing population on a finite planet and so limiting the speed of growth is a good idea. Now that the planet has gone beyond seven billion people and is likely to reach nine billion by 2050, there is a growing realisation that action needs to be taken[9].

However, population growth is not the major cause of the current crisis and it's unfair to blame the countries with a faster growing population for the current crisis. The main cause is how much we consume and how the things we consume are made. So that's why we are in this mess. We want too much stuff thinking that it will bring happiness. The stuff we have has been produced in the wrong way and yet despite this we want to carry on having more and more of it.

Chapter 2

How are Christians reacting to this challenge?

1. We just don't think

At the heart of the problem is the fact that most Christians have just not given much thought to the impact their lives have on the rest of God's creation or to what God's Word has to say about ecological issues. Time and time again when I talk to Christians about creation care all I get is puzzled looks and a conversation about recycling. At a wedding I attended recently I talked to a leading evangelical pastor about creation care and as I spoke he stroked his chin and confessed that he hadn't given the matter much thought. The same words came from an elder in another church and from other Christians at the wedding. I hope I didn't spoil the day by serious conversation but let me say it again: it appears that many Christians have simply not thought about the relationship between their faith and a distinctive creation care witness.

The sad truth is that most Christians simply are not aware of the impact that we have on the earth and so we don't think about what God's Word has to say about creation and ecological issues. Although most Christians would probably accept that God's creation is under threat and that climate change is a reality, they would also freely admit that they haven't really given the issues a huge amount of biblical thinking time. Most of us carry on our lives without asking how our lifestyles have an impact on creation and whether this or that action is one that a Christian should really be doing.

It appears that both as individual Christians and as a worldwide Church we are relatively unconcerned with the fact that we seem to be indistinguishable from the rest of the population in terms of our apparent lack of active concern and care for creation. This lack of knowledge, lack of thinking and consequent lack of action is somewhat puzzling. The Church actively seeks to be salt and light (Matthew 5:13-14) in so many areas of society such as campaigning against poverty of the trafficking of women, and not only that, works to provide practical solutions. When it comes to creation care we appear to shed no light and spread no salt!

Christians, have the perfectly normal human characteristic of focusing on the here and now and on the issues that affect us locally. Because many of the problems facing God's creation are not experienced first-hand it is easy to put thoughts of action towards the back of our minds. We want to get on with more immediate matters. We pray for Christians in Africa affected by drought and malnutrition but perhaps we often forget to pray for ourselves as part of the problem. We help through supporting a Christian charity that will feed and educate malnourished children but do we think that part of the cause might be our impact on climate and our own demand for cheap food? We are concerned when we hear about the poor working conditions of the young people making our t-shirts in China and maybe we pray them. But do we realise that the answer to our prayers lies in a change in our consumer behaviour? Employers could pay their workers higher wages and give them better working conditions if we were willing to pay more for our clothes.

Christians should know about these things. The problem is that the tremendous amount of information on our current ecological crisis can be overwhelming and decisions seem so complicated and so we take the easiest way out and carry on as before. When we do take some meaningful action it often takes hard work and sometimes money, for seemingly little, if any, personal gain. Too many of us are perhaps like Hezekiah who when told that some of his descendants would suffer as a result of his disobedience thought 'Phew – at least everything will be fine in my lifetime!' (2 Kings 20.19). We find it tough to think about doing something now to help stop some possible global disaster in the future especially if we don't quite believe in it. Maybe younger people don't think this way, but they can also be disheartened by small actions that don't seem to make a difference. It is far easier to blame the older generation for the mess and still carry on as before!

This might seem a little unfair. It isn't that Christians aren't active, it's just that we don't do enough, or do it distinctively. Most Christians demonstrate care for creation by joining in with society at large in 'doing our bit' to help the earth, taking part in accepted environmental behaviours such as recycling, composting, using energy saving lamps, perhaps buying organic and fair trade food, not using plastic bags and so on. Those slightly more ecologically enthusiastic Christians might also try and use their car less and cycle instead, perhaps use more public transport and maybe even purchase green electricity. However, very few Christians go further to be "bright green", as it were. There is certainly a lack of visible Christian ecological witness. Like the rest of the western population, most Christians feel happy enough with a low level of commitment and action. Recycling, yes and it's easy. Giving up flying on a foreign holiday? Well, that might be more of a challenge.

It might be uncomfortable to realise that Christians have not given much faith-focused thought to the key issues. It's not that Christians don't care, it is simply that we haven't given much consideration to the relationship between our faith and ecological, climate change issues or how to demonstrate that faith in practical ways. This theological laziness is not for any perverse reason; it's just that having a Christian perspective on environmental issues hasn't yet struck home to most believers as being important. The result is that many Christians are not particularly well informed about ecological issues either theologically or practically. Unfortunately, this is especially prevalent amongst Church leaders. Like the Pharisees in John 9, we seem spiritually blind

This unbelieving and unthinking position is untenable. Christians have a responsibility to think about every issue that has an impact on the creation of which we are a part. Twenty first century society is incredibly complex and the number of challenges that Christians face in terms of the application of our faith is growing exponentially, but that is no excuse. God wants us to be a thinking people using our heart and mind in his world.

2. God is in control so it doesn't matter what we do

God holds everything together - everything is in his hands. This is clear throughout the Bible, most gloriously in Psalm 104, a song of praise to our creating and upholding God. We can trust that God is managing what happens on his earth and we can trust that he is managing it for his glory. We do not need to be wracked by despair about the future because we are told throughout the Bible that God created this earth and that he and his Son hold all things together. No matter how much we might beat and batter God's creation he is in control. He manages his creation and directly controls all things and sees all things. Although it is difficult for Christians to understand how God does this, and even more difficult to explain when so called natural disasters strike, it is an immense source of comfort and strength. Christians can be crystal clear that God is in control, and holds everything together not matter what mess we make of his creation. The result of this belief is that in one way we don't have to

56

be worried about the future. Having said that we don't know whether God will keep his creation exactly as it is for all time because he has not told us the details. What he has told us is that He is in undisputed sovereign control and that the end of this present world is also in his hands (Psalm 104 and 2 Peter 3). That's what we need to hold on to.

But that does not mean that we should not care about it? Of course not! What kind of logic is that? It doesn't mean that we can sit back and think, 'Oh well, God is in charge, let's leave it all to him and we can do what we like'. That is not what God has commanded us to do. He has given us certain clear responsibilities and as Christians we know perfectly well that we cannot sin as we like knowing that God will forgive that sin. We don't just sit back and say about other issues such as poverty, war, child abuse, corruption, starvation, 'oh it doesn't matter, God is in control', so why should we use this argument when it comes to the damage we are doing to the rest of creation? As Christians we care. Just as we try and do something about these social and political issues here and now instead of waiting until the end of time, so we should be concerned about ecological challenges and climate change. We should work hard to do something about them whilst at the same time knowing that the Creator is in control. Despite the ecological mantra "The earth is in our hands", we know that at the most important level, it is not. Thankfully God is in charge, but that can never be an excuse for inaction.

3. Why don't Christians do more?

Christians hold a variety of views that are sometimes given to explain a lack of serious faith focused thought about creation care and these are considered below. There are specific responses to each one of these but it important to note at the start of this chapter that there is a thread linking them all together. Few Christians would dare give these reasons to explain a lack of Christian intervention in other endeavours to make God's world a better place. These excuses are an example of the kind of back to front thinking that my son Tom and I discussed during the writing of this book. For example, we would not use any of these reasons above to justify a lack of Christian action on combating poverty, protecting children from abuse, helping those in real need, or the many other issues that Christians are rightly involved in. We don't use these reasons to explain a lack of action on social issues of direct concern to humans and they should not be accepted as a lack of creation concern either. Is caring for creation any less important than taking action in these areas? Although some Christians might answer "yes", the Biblical response is "not at all!"

Evangelism is more important than creation care

The main task of any Christian is to glorify God and demonstrate this is through the way we live our lives. One common reason given for less than enthusiastic involvement in creation care is that the main task of a Christian is to work as hard as possible to bring other people to Christ. This is what glorifies God, not spending time tackling ecological challenges. It is right that some Christians should be more involved, but it isn't for everyone. We know that the core of the good news of salvation is not caring for creation. People become Christians when they realise their sin and the position this puts them in before God. However, as we shall see, a lack of creation care is actually sin. In our pursuit of holiness therefore, it is should not be a choice between either "evangelism" or "caring for creation"; it is both and we need to realise the links between the two! Whilst it is true that God does not require everyone to be politically involved and actively campaigning on ecological issues, there is a fundamental level of obedience that is required of all

Christians which is inescapable - discipleship involves giving our whole lives to Christ.

Our ecological crisis is the judgement of God

Some Christians also suggest that our current ecological crisis, or at least some of the effects of it, are a result of the judgement of God. We know that God has total control of nature and that in biblical times he used natural disasters such as droughts and resulting famines to show his displeasure and to punish (for example 2 Samuel 21:1 or 24:13). We know that both in the Old and New Testament God demonstrated his power through demonstrating his control over so called natural events, but is this how God works today? Are "natural disasters" a judgement of God? Is God allowing people to change the climate also his judgement?

Contrary to the impression given by the media, relatively few people are affected by natural disasters compared with the thousands upon thousands of people who die each day because of disasters created by humans. Just think of the 25,000 children who die each day as a result of malnutrition and water-borne disease even when solutions are available for both. Although it is true that there are the huge disasters such as tsunami, earthquakes, droughts and hurricanes which have no human cause at all and which often cause large numbers of deaths and the destruction of homes, hospitals and schools, can they be said to be the result of God's judgement?

This is a difficult issue and one to be approached with caution. We know that God is in control and throughout the history of the Old Testament we see God directly punishing his people and others through famine and other disasters. However, it is important to note that God did not send these judgements without a warning to the people. The link between disobedience and disaster, whether it be famine or storm, was known in every case and God's use of natural events in punishment was made clear to the people affected. This was also true in the case of rewards. For example, the whole of Deuteronomy chapter 11 describes the blessings that will follow obedience when the people of Israel enter the land God promised them (Deuteronomy 11:13-15). We can see how God used natural events to both punish and bless when he spoke to Solomon. "When I shut up the heavens so that there is no rain, or command locusts to devour the land or send a plague among my people, if my people, who are called by my name, will humble themselves and pray and seek my face and turn from their wicked ways, then will I hear from heaven and will forgive their sin and will heal their land." (2 Chronicles 7:13–14).

Today things are both the same and different. God has not changed. He controls his creation in the same way that he always has done - he has that same infinite power. The difference is that God does not speak to his people in the same way. The days of the Old Testament prophets are long gone and, although disasters still continue, we have no certain way of knowing whether a particular event is or isn't the judgement of God. Even trying to work it out is a fruitless activity and is missing the point. We know that God is sovereign and will judge everyone at the end of time. We know that God can and does judge people today, but beyond that knowledge, trying to work out what is and what is not the judgement of God is neither helpful nor possible. Whether an environmental disaster is or is not the punishment of God is not the main issue. An earthquake strikes and destroys homes and lives, and as Christians we don't just sit back and say, "Well, it's the judgement of God" and carry on reading our Bibles. No, we demonstrate care to those caught up in the disaster through praying, giving and working – all in the light of God's sovereign grace. It might or might not be judgement but that's not for us to debate or decide.

What is critical is how we react as Christians and how we live our lives before Christ comes again.

When Christ returns there will be a new heaven and new earth

Some Christians also believe that it doesn't really matter how we treat this world as when Christ comes again there will be a new heaven and earth (2 Peter 3:13). Whilst this might be a logical assumption from a human point of view it is far from God's logic. Peter's second letter has a lot to say about the end of time, and although it is not the purpose of this book to consider the second coming of Christ and what will happen to the earth in any great detail, it is worth noting a few points. The most important fact is that Christ is coming again, and while our view of the future should determine how a Christian lives in the present, to think that it doesn't matter how we treat God's creation just because one day it will be all made new is terribly flawed theology. We know that creation is groaning in anticipation of his coming again (Romans 8:22) but we don't have the right to make it groan more than it is already. God's Word in relation to how the future affects our present behaviour focuses on two areas.

Firstly, God will one day return as judge and we should therefore be motivated towards greater holiness and walk more and more in the way Jesus walked (2 Peter 3:11-12). In fact, in these verses Peter states that we should live 'holy and godly lives as you look forward to the day of God to speed its coming'. If we consider that our lack of creation care is a sin, then becoming more like Jesus in our ecological behaviour is all part and parcel of holiness. To speed Christ's coming we should demonstrate our creation care. Surely we should want Christ's world to be as perfect as possible when he returns? Secondly, we should not be living for the things of this world. We are 'in the world but not of the world' (John 15:19), which suggests that creation damaging lifestyles are really not what we should desire and seek after. Creation caring ones are! Time and time again God tells us of the worthlessness of the stuff that weighs us down in our twenty-first century lifestyles and that hinders our Christian race (Hebrews 12:1). Isn't it time we took him seriously?

We don't know exactly what the new heavens and new earth will look like just as we don't know what our new bodies will look like. The way the new heavens and new earth are described in the Bible is very interesting. The words are the same the as the words for 'new self' and 'new creation' used to describe people when they become Christians. This leads many people to conclude that earth won't be destroyed by fire at the end of time, but restored or made new in some way that we can't describe. We know that creation is groaning for that time, groaning in anticipation and possibly groaning as in the pains of childbirth. We know too that when Christ comes again in his final act of faithfulness and redemption, that this groaning will end (Romans 8:22). Our challenge in relating to creation before the end of time can be compared with how we relate to people. Until Christ comes again our duty is to work hard to alleviate physical and spiritual groaning. So it is with the rest of God's creation that we belong to. We should be working hard to alleviate creation's groaning too. We can't undo the effects of the fall either for people or the rest of creation, but we can work to bring both nearer to the paradise once experienced in Eden.

We are just doing what God told us to do

Another reason why some Christians are not too worried about the damage being done to creation is because they feel that they are only obeying God's command to Adam in Genesis to 'subdue the earth' (Genesis 1:28). If this obedience results in problems then they put their trust in technology and human ingenuity to come up with solutions before it's too late. And if it is already too late then that doesn't matter for a Christian anyway. There is nothing to worry about! The same people often exhort us not to worry because there is plenty of evidence that natural systems, given time, can recover from human damage. These points are true up to a point. Many systems can recover from the damage we inflict on them and it is also true that technologies are available to both solve the problems and give us a better quality of life. But surely these are not excuses for causing the problems in the first place. It's like saying that child abuse is acceptable because God has provided people and organisations to help children recover from the experience! This is a ridiculous notion. Instead we should be thankful to God for giving us the people who can invent technologies that offer solutions to the mess we are making. This is yet another sign of his grace, but not something we can rely on to happen forever!

This has been a long chapter and it is worth repeating that all these reasons for not caring for creation are untenable. Although the arguments to some extent sound very plausible and even spiritual, none of them really wash when compared with what God tells us in his Word and how He expects us to think and act. Yes,

God is in control of the earth; yes, things have changed in the past; yes, our main task should be to evangelise; yes, God given technologies will help; yes, God has promised not to destroy the world again until the end of time and, finally; yes, He is coming again in glory and power. But none of these are reasons why we shouldn't reflect the care that God has for his own creation.

4. The whole environmental movement puts me off

Many Christians are put off by the thought that being 'ecological' means being associated with the likes of Greenpeace or Friends of the Earth or at the very least living an odd ecological lifestyle growing a beard and having organic muesli or lentils for breakfast, lunch and dinner! There is a perception that being ecological is a costly lifestyle. However, if obeying the Word of God means being seen to be at odds with the society as a whole and behaving differently, then this is precisely what Christians are expected to do. We also need to consider that no matter how those groups are perceived, the ecological footprints of their members are probably about half the size of most Christians – something that should challenge us surely?

As with so many issues, it is important that we don't let the behaviour of others distract us from what God wants us to do. Again, all sorts of different groups are involved in campaigning for social justice, but we don't let that stop us working with them on issues like abortion, human rights, and poverty alleviation. In the same way our job is to claim ecological living for Christ and not be put off by the sometimes slightly odd lifestyles of the minority of non-Christian environmentalists. In any case, the image of the bearded, lentil eating, tree-worshipping ecologist is very far from the truth. There are many environmental organisations that are much more mainstream and 'respectable' than this stereotype. These include green business groups, political organisations, campaigning groups such as WWF, green bankers, as well as the civil servants who develop national and local government policies and even some church leaders! Being ecologically conscious is becoming far more accepted these days and the 'eco freak' image is fast becoming history. But if obeying God's creation care commands means that you might appear strange to your neighbours as you get rid of your second car, start cycling a lot more and perhaps forgo that summer holiday in a distant destination, then so be it. Beards of course are optional, but in many ways that kind of behaviour is no odder to our neighbours than spending time inside on a bright sunny Sunday singing songs and listening to someone talk about God! We are more than happy to do this each week! Caring for creation is no different from believing that sex should be saved for marriage which most people in our society would think distinctly odd. Let's not mind then if following God's creation commands make us look a little odd too!

Christians do need to be careful though. More importantly than the way in which many environmentalists look and behave are the driving beliefs some hold that no Christian could agree with. There are, for example, the "deep ecologists" who would say that "all living things have an equal right to life". Whilst this is patently not true and few environmentalists live as if it was, the belief when stated is rarely challenged and influences both policy and actions. Then there is the Gaia Theory of James Lovelock which holds that the earth is a kind of huge 'living organism' and responds to human damage much as a body might to a virus or disease. There are also those who take a more mystical approach to creation and those with so called 'New Age' beliefs that suggest a return to the way in which tribal people live close to the land and worship 'Mother Earth' through a variety of weird and wonderful festivals. Add all these together and we have a set of very good reasons why Bible believing Christians might want to think twice before 'getting involved' with such groups. That's not to say we shouldn't try and influence them, but it is no wonder some Christians find 'being environmental' difficult. Be that as it may, we need to be brave and reclaim ecological living for Christ. To adapt a famous quote, 'Why should the Devil have all the best ecological living ideas?'

Then there is the thorny perception that 'being environmental' is a costly lifestyle, only to be afforded by those with a high enough income to buy into the organic, fair trade and local shopping dream! It is undeniable that ecological products are sometimes more expensive. Not always, but often, the same basket of goods grown or made in a way that does not damage the planet is going to be more expensive than those that are. That's the strange way the world works, at least for the moment. But, before we decide that we can't afford creation care lifestyles we need to consider a number of factors.

Of course, if you buy the things that you usually buy, but made in a creation caring way, then life is likely to be more expensive. But who said you need to buy the same things? Shopping ecologically might mean might mean buying fewer meat products and more seasonal vegetables, or one T shirt made from organic cotton rather than three made in a way that destroys creation. This might sound like bad news, but Christians should be happy to change behaviour to become more holy. We shouldn't really count the financial cost of obedience, should we? In any case, it's not all bad news. Things will change. As more people demand more ecological goods, prices will come down, maybe not to the levels of our really cheap products at the moment, but certainly lower than they are now.

Of course, I don't know the circumstances of every person reading this book and not everyone will have the same choices and opportunities. It is easy to say that if obedience to God's command about creation care means doing without some things and spending more money on others, then this is how it needs to be. This may sound harsh and unsympathetic, especially to those who don't have high levels of disposable income, and I don't want to be unfair. That having been said, generally we have too much stuff – food, clothes, electronic goods, holidays – everything. We have them because by and large, they are cheap and easily available. If we spent the same amount of money and had fewer things would that really be so terrible? There are also all those small things our grandparents did that we have forgotten how to do, such as using leftovers, growing our own food, repairing clothes (or even making our own), turning things off when they are not being used. These things take time, but since when did obedience to God depend on how much time we had available?

An ecological lifestyle is possible at a reasonable cost if we are willing, for God, to make those readjustments. And that's the key question, isn't it? How much are we really willing to change?

5. What about the Church?

It needs to be said that the Church must take some of the responsibility for the lack of creation care thinking and action. Although we have an individual responsibility before God for how we live, God has given us the Church as a family in which to grow and be fed and nurtured spiritually. Caring for creation and ecological living should be at the heart of being a Christian disciple and it is sad that so little teaching is heard and so little leadership is given on this by the local churches. There are some positive signs. Certain groups of churches are becoming more awake to the need for creation care teaching than others and there is a growing amount of Christian literature covering ecological issues, not to mention a growing number of Christian ecological organisations to join. Some of these are listed at the end of the book. Having said that, ecological living is not often a topic for debate in most of our Churches.

Over the last few years a lot of attention has been given to the creation/evolution debate, which you would have thought would have flowed easily into discourse about caring for creation. However, energies have been focused on defending a theological and scientific argument for creation as a process rather than taking the next logical step and applying our belief in a creator God through demonstrating more positive care for that creation.

Conversely, creation care is a relatively new issue for Christians to consider. Although there were visionaries in the nineteenth century who spoke out against the damage people were causing to planet earth, it has only been over the past fifty years or so that the true depth of what we have done to God's creation has become apparent. Whilst generally giving excellent biblical teaching in relation to creation and our expected loving stewardship of God's natural gifts, church leaders of a hundred years ago can perhaps be excused for not giving practical advice to back up their biblical teaching. Most of the ecological issues that we face today were not really a problem and at those times there were other social, political and economic issues for the Church to deal with. The concept of climate change and human action as the cause of global catastrophes may have been outside the field of comprehension of Christian leaders at that time.

We are living in a fully blown consumer society that has its roots in the industrial revolution of the eighteenth century when the mass production of cheap goods gave more people the opportunity to own things that previously only the very rich could possess. At this time little thought was given to the resources being used. It was assumed that natural things such as forests for fuel, soil for growing food, seas and rivers for fish, rocks for minerals and later coal and oil for energy were all inexhaustible. It was thought that we could consume as much as possible because these resources were either going to be around for the rest of time, or replenish themselves for our benefit. The idea that over using them was also causing some damage to creation was something that had not really crossed people's minds. Any local issues of concern were not put down to a global effect.

Now things are different. The lack of Church leadership in the past may be forgiven, but God is giving us a new understanding of his creation so that we can meet the urgent ecological challenges we are facing. The Church has a responsibility to take this new knowledge about our impact on the planet and hold it up to the light of the Word of God so that we may take our guidance and instructions from him. Whilst some leaders have spoken out consistently, creation care is still far from being a mainstream part of church life[10].

Some individual Christians and churches perceive that the Christian environmental movement has been influenced by non-Christian thinking and action. This can be discouraging, but it should be seen as an opportunity for evangelical Christians to get involved. We can make changes and join that growing number of Christians who are convinced of the need get more involved and be more active.

Chapter 3

God and creation – what the Bible says

1. A new Christian understanding

The idea of creation care and a Christian ecological perspective is in many ways a new one. Many Christians, especially those of a reformed background, might find the whole idea of new insights into the meaning of God's Word more than a little unsettling. Some points in response to this unease have been covered in previous chapters but it is worth considering a few more. If creation care is so important why haven't we thought about it much before? Why the emphasis now?

It is well known that our behaviour is determined by the frameworks or ways of thinking we construct about a whole range of subjects. Putting it another way, our behaviour is influenced by our 'world view', which for a Christian should be based on the Bible. These deep rooted frameworks are difficult to change and so when new ideas come along then if they don't fit the frame we already have, they are usually rejected rather than the framework of ideas being adapted. Everyone has these frameworks that are sometimes so powerful that even sound biblical arguments cannot easily shift them. Christians are finding it difficult to let go of the traditional frameworks about creation and creation care outlined partly because the new ideas don't appear to fit with current beliefs. As a result, they are rejected, sometimes without being given much serious thought. This chapter is a plea for us to be willing to change our Christian framing of issues, something that some Christians can be reluctant to do.

God's Word reveals to us all we need to know about our salvation and our relationships with him, with other people, and with his creation for all time. There is nothing more to add. However, I also firmly believe that Christians develop a specific understanding of what God is saying to us to meet needs of a society at a particular time and that God directs this understanding. When God's Word was first spoken the people who heard it didn't always have a full and immediate understanding of what God was saying. Just think of the disciples. They were with Jesus during his lifetime on earth and yet their understanding of his mission and their roles in it took time to grow. Time after time Jesus gently chided them for their lack of understanding and then taught them (Luke 9:45, 18:34, 24:45). Similarly, our understanding is always growing and maturing -

what Paul calls the transformation of our minds (Romans 12:2). It's important to realise that this transformation is a process, not a destination. It can take a long time as our understanding grows through the guidance of his Spirit.

For example, up until around 1750, most Christians hadn't given much thought to the issue of slavery and some even justified the slavery well into the twentieth century. In the late eighteenth and early nineteenth centuries, William Wilberforce and others changed all that by being given a better understanding what God's Word said about individuals enslaving other human beings. Through his efforts the law was changed in the United Kingdom and then country by country, across the world. Two hundred years on, the concept of slavery now fills us with disgust. Ecology and climate change are amongst the huge challenges of today and thankfully through the Holy Spirit we are being given a better understanding of what God is telling us about our relationship to the rest of his creation. Christian involvement in social issues has always been strong and historically God has raised up those skilled in explaining what God expects from his people. He has brought us practitioners with the skills to put God's Word and care into action in areas such as caring for the family, helping those in poverty and many others. Christians have led from the front in many issues but it is only recently that creation care has been amongst them. Now, I believe God is raising up people to encourage Christians in this area. If we believe this it is exciting to think that we are part of God's plan to protect and save his precious creation. He doesn't want people to engage in the destruction of the earth he has created. Rather he wants us to be part of his plan to care for it! What a thought!

Because theologians haven't said much about our relationship with creation until recently, we are not familiar with these new ideas and, as a result, some of the things we read and some of the language used might jar a little. This is not because the ideas are wrong, but because they are new. If you feel like this, please be patient. Go to the Bible, look at the some of the passages about creation care, and ask yourself 'What is God really saying here?' Don't assume that what you think the verses said last time you read them is the final word, but instead consider what it says in relation to this topic now?

The word of God never changes and is eternally true. At the same time, however, God is continually giving us greater insights into his Word, allowing us to live in contemporary society and develop our understanding of him. Christians have a huge responsibility to constantly ask ourselves – is our interpretation of the Bible and how we put it into practice 'right'?

2. God created the earth

The Bible opens with the words, 'In the beginning God created the heavens and the earth' (Genesis 1:1). It is worth just sitting still for a few moments and reflecting on the fact that God created the earth and all that is in it, and then meditating on the implications of God's infinite creating power. It is not the aim of this book to explore all the issues around creation and evolution or what the earth will look like when Christ comes again. Both debates often miss the point of creation. Our God is so powerful, so wonderful, he could have created the earth in six milliseconds. Six days of twenty-four hours is actually a long time for an infinitely powerful God! The purpose of this book is to look at how we are treating God's earth in the time between the creating act recorded in Genesis and the time when Jesus returns. A belief in a creating God is the fundamental starting point for creation care and it is the starting point that makes for a distinctive Christian witness.

The whole of creation belongs to God. On a cosmic scale it is his earth, not ours (Psalm 24:1) and we are his tenants and stewards (Leviticus 23:24 - 25). The same is true at a local scale. The place we live in is his, not ours. He created the earth and all that is in it and at the end of the process he declared that what he had done was "very good". We are told in Hebrews that we believe this through faith (11:3). Before the fall creation was perfect, and although Adam's first sin brought this perfection to an end, and subsequently our unthinking behaviour as a human race has added to that, God can still be seen in creation. It still belongs to him. It is still wonderful and he still cares for it, as he still cares for us despite our sin. Because of our sin we also know that creation is groaning in expectation until Jesus comes again and we know that the world in its present form will pass away (Romans 8:22).

Two of the most fundamental issues we can question are, 'why was this world created?' and 'why we are here?' After all, God did not have to create the earth or put people on it. He is God, a unique and independent being and doesn't need an earth or people to exist. Although there is no clear answer in Genesis, in Isaiah 45:18 we are told that God did not create the earth to be empty but made it to be inhabited. Furthermore, in

Psalm 115:16 we are that 'the earth he has given to man'. Quite obviously the earth is ours! But that is by no means the whole story. Paul writes some amazing words in his letter to the church in Colossae. In Colossians 1:15-20 Paul is teaching the church about the supremacy of Christ and he starts by saying, 'For by him were all things created' (Colossians 1:16). In other words, God and Christ were working together in creation. John starts his gospel by saying the same thing in those magnificent words, "In the beginning was the Word, and the Word was with God and the Word was God. He was with God in the beginning. Through him all things were made; without him nothing was made that was made' (John 1:1-3).

Paul continues with the incredible words that "all things were created by him and for him". Notice those last two words – "for him". Here we are clearly told that whole of creation was not only made by Jesus, but also for Jesus. Although we are not told why, just knowing this is fantastic enough. Meditating deeply and fully on this verse would be a good starting point in thinking about creation care.

This wonderful earth was created both by Jesus and for Jesus. It was also created for us. That's why we exist. The whole of creation belongs to Jesus and to us and we belong to Jesus. Why God did things this way is a mystery but one we should praise Him for as the psalmists did on many occasions. Psalm 24 says the same thing and it is one of those truths woven throughout the Bible. Creation was made by God, belongs to God, and is under God's control. If only Christians spent time meditating on what that really means in terms on a personal level it would surely be enough to spur us on to live ecological lives.

We are an intimate part of creation. Human beings were created by God and although we are very different from the other elements of creation there is no escaping we are part of it. We are different and special because we were created in God's image (Genesis 1:27) and this brings with it so many characteristics that are not shared with the animals which were created 'according to their kind' (Genesis 1:25). It was one of these unique characteristics - our desire for wisdom - that got humans into trouble with God in the first place. We are different because both Adam and Eve were created from something, the dust of the earth and the rib of man (Genesis 2:7 and 2:21-22). We are different because we can communicate with and know God. God spoke directly to Adam and Eve in the Garden of Eden. So, although we are different to animals in many, many reasons, we are still an intimate part of that creation and share so much with it.

Perhaps as a result of the creation and evolution debate we find it hard to admit that we have so much in common with the animals that God created. However, we are told in Genesis that when Adam needed a partner he first looked to the animals to find one (Genesis 2:20)! He failed, and so God created Eve, but we should not forget that Adam first searched amongst the animals, naming them as he did so. Surely these facts speak of our oneness with creation. Phrases such as "oneness with creation" can often sound more like a Native American Indian or Buddhist philosophy, but really it is highly biblical and nothing to be afraid of! The implications of this oneness are huge. In our minds we often think of 'humans and creation' as being separate entities. This is not a biblical position to take. When the Bible talks of "all creation" as Paul does in that glorious part of his letter to the Colossians (Colossians 1:15-16), the meaning of the word 'creation' he uses includes human beings and animals and plants altogether. Sometimes God does not conceptually separate His living creation in the way that we do!

Therefore, when we damage this creation it's serious. God made this earth and made it with his Son and for his Son. What right do we have to damage something specifically made by God, and what's more, made specifically for Jesus and given to us as a gift? There is only one answer. We have no right at all. You wouldn't knowingly damage a gift you were given; so why do we behave the same way with creation? Well do I remember breaking a precious ornament in the house of a wonderful Christian couple where I was leading a young peoples' meeting. It was an ornament given by the husband to his wife to symbolise their love and commitment to each other. The guilt was huge and I could not really rest until I had confessed to the damage and then sought out an exact replacement. Is that how we feel about God's gift of creation to His Son? Unfortunately, we are more likely to behave like Adam and Eve when they first sinned when they tried to hide from God in the Garden of Eden!

We also need to remember that we are not damaging something that is separate from our being, but damaging something we are intimately connected with. If we pollute the soil then we polluting that from which we were made! I am not saying that humans and God's natural world are worthy of equal care. This is not true.

Jesus says clearly in Luke 12:24 that humans are more important than animals and plants. What I am saying is that our close relationship with creation is something that needs more thought. It gives us both rights and responsibilities.

3. What is the purpose of creation?

Creation belongs to God, we are an intimate part of creation, and we were created by God and for Jesus. But creation also has other purposes!

The first is to feed us, support us and provide for our needs. In Genesis, God tells us more than once that he has provided plants as food for His whole creation (Genesis 1:9). Throughout the rest of his word we are told of the other things God has created that are provided for our use such as water to drink, trees for fuel and shelter, minerals for metals and so on. They are all there for us to use legitimately, and all provided freely to Christians and non-Christians alike as part of God's common grace. God has promised to provide for our needs through the rest of His creation. It should also be pointed out that God has provided these things in abundance. We should keep in mind that our God is not a mean God! Solomon realised this when he became what was possibly the world's first recorded ecologist in 1 Kings 4:33, where his knowledge of creation is counted alongside other characteristics of his great wisdom

The second purpose of creation is to give us pleasure. In Genesis, God also says that his creation is 'pleasing to the eye' (Genesis 2:9). Although this verse talks specifically about trees, there is no doubt that this applies to creation as whole. Creation is beautiful, for us to wonder at and take pleasure in. This is one of the reasons why most people experience a wide range of emotions such as peace, exhilaration, wonder, and joy when out in the countryside.

Thirdly, God's creation communicates something about its creator. There are so many places in the Bible where we are told that creation declares God's glory and wonder. The writer of Psalm 19 states, 'the heavens declare the glory of God, skies proclaim the work of his hands: Day after day they pour forth speech; night after night they display knowledge' (Psalm 19:1-2). Christians can wonder at their mighty and powerful God who created all we see from the stars at night to the smallest insects. Throughout the Bible God tells us that his creation communicates his glory to people that have not heard him preached (Romans 1:20). Indeed, for those people who have not heard the message of good news directly it is the only way for them to find out about God and his greatness.

Therefore, when we harm God's creation it is serious. It's not like breaking something around the house that perhaps can be mended or replaced. We are damaging the ability of creation to do each of the things God designed it to do as part of his common grace to all people. Yes, it is true that we can 'mend' creation to some extent, but only if we are aware that the damage we have caused is serious enough for us to care. Even if creation can be repaired, the very fact of breaking it in the first places demonstrates that we hold a specific set of values which highlight a lack of care. We have damaged the ability of God's creation to fulfil its purposes. Having an impact on just one of the purposes of creation is bad enough but humans appear to be doing our best to spoil all of them!

The population of the earth is over seven billion people and is predicted to rise to between nine and ten billion by 2050[11]. Feeding this number of people is already a daily challenge in some countries and it is going to get harder each year as population grows. We can be thankful to God that we have, on the whole, managed to feed this growing number of people but it is still to our global shame that so many people, especially children, die of starvation and suffer from malnutrition when God has provided us an abundance of food and water. If there was not enough food in the world this situation would be sad enough, but in a world where God has given us plenty it is unforgivable. The problem lies not with the total population but with how the food we have at the moment is distributed between everyone. This unfair system is partly a result of the way food production and consumption has been organised globally to favour some people and some countries more than others.

Another sad fact is that in the richer well fed countries of the world, where few people go really hungry each day, wasting food each day appears to be a common activity. We also need to consider the sin of our over consumption of food. Recent research in Europe suggests that up to 35% of food produced is wasted through processing and supermarket practices and the growing obesity and diabetes challenges point to the effects of our overconsumption. A consideration of these statistics can only lead to the conclusion that we are using valuable farm land to grow food we will eventually throw away or eat to the point of unhealthiness[12]. Other issues associated with food production include the fact that three quarters of the world's fish stocks are overfished and the way that we have treated the soil through the use of fertiliser and pesticide is now reducing yield and capacity instead of increasing it. This situation a sad reflection of our human condition, but through our climate changing activities we are adding insult to injury by undermining the capacity of the earth to grow the food we need in the future. Higher temperatures are already reducing the yield of basic crops such as rice, and changes to water tables and growing seasons are going to result in more negative impacts in the future. It needs to be emphasised that although we cannot recreate Eden, there could be plentiful food for all. Our God is still a wonderfully generous God and holds the earth together so that this food can be provided in abundance.

But it is not only the supply of food we are putting at risk though our lack of creation care. We are also destroying the evidence of his glory. What right do we have to reduce the capacity of creation to teach us about our creator God and even worse, reduce the ability of creation to communicate something about God to people who have not heard? In fact, if we want to be tough with ourselves, we could be accused of making it more difficult for people to see God through creation. That must be serious! In Luke 12 Jesus used creation to illustrate God's care for His people, encouraging those listening to consider the birds flying around him as he spoke and the flowers in the field he was standing in. God cares for them, he explains, so how much more will he care for you! If Jesus returned to some parts of his world today he might be hard pushed to see enough birds and flowers to use as illustrations for his message. Although thankfully through God's grace, there is still enough of the beauty and wonder of creation around to show the world the glory of God, but climate change and other human activity is reducing the natural beauty on the earth at an unimaginable rate.

In our heart of hearts we all know this. In much of Europe we live in a completely managed landscape, but we can still feel awe and wonder when we are walking in the mountains, or an old beech forest, or by a fast moving river. It is sad that our deluded and greedy lifestyles are causing the destruction of just these kinds of beautiful habitats in other countries. We work hard to protect our own natural environment but, perhaps unknowingly, seem to care so little for God's creation in other countries. For example, it is our desire for mobile phones and other electronics that has led to wholesale destruction of rainforests in the Congo where companies mine for one ingredient that is used in most electronic products, coltan. The mining of another ingredient, gold, is causing huge environmental destruction in other countries of Africa. This destruction is doubly sad because it is in these countries that many people have not heard the good news preached. God's creation is all they have, and we are taking that away from them![13]

If our feelings tell us that God can be seen in creation then this will be the feeling of people who have yet to hear the good news. God has been gracious enough in his power to make sure that his creation is still beautiful and can still tell people of his glory, but that is evidence of his sustaining power rather than anything we have done. We should be hanging our heads in shame at this point, but not for long! The word of God covers every area of our lives and of course God hasn't left us without guidance about how he wants us to look after his world!

4. Caring for creation - what is said in Genesis?

Our responsibilities towards creation are given in three key sections of God's word. In Genesis chapters 1 and 2, God uses five different words and phrases to describe how he wants us to behave towards the rest of his creation: 'rule over' (1:26), 'subdue' (1:28), 'work', (2:15) 'take care' (2:15), 'increase in number' and 'fill' the earth (1:28). Each of these words carries with them a group of earthly meanings, but our task is to mirror what these words mean to God and the way we can see him carrying them out.

Before going into detail about each of the responsibilities given there are some general points to consider. The first thing we should remember is that they have all been given to us as humans created in the image of God and 'in our likeness' (Genesis 1:26). As a result, it is safe to assume that God expects us to carry out these responsibilities in the way that God would do them. Secondly, it is also worth remembering that these responsibilities can be seen as creation ordinances, just as much as for example, God resting on the seventh day means Christians should also have a day of rest and consider it holy. As creation ordinances, ruling over, subduing, working caring for and filling the earth are not optional or negotiable. But they do have to be understood properly. It is also worth noting that these responsibilities were given to humans before the fall. Much as we might not like the word "subdue" for example, as today's meaning can seem slightly negative, it was something that God expected of Adam before sin entered the world. It can therefore only have a positive meaning. The fall broke the relationships between God and humans, between God and creation and between humans and creation. Although the process of reconciliation started immediately after the fall we have instructions here about how God expects us to behave to work towards that reconciliation. All the words are also linked together and cannot be taken in isolation. We cannot 'rule over' without 'caring for' for creation. We cannot 'care for' without 'working' creation. As so often is the case, trouble comes to our Christian lives when we pick and choose God's commands. Finally, all these words give people the responsibility of managing creation on behalf of God, not instead of God. God has not just given us creation and then walked away. It is a gift we have to treasure. It is a gift that the maker is still intimately involved with.

The first word God uses is the instruction to **"rule over"** all creatures over all the earth, or 'have dominion over' in older translations of the Bible (Genesis 1:25). These are familiar words but it is important to think carefully about what exactly they mean because it is very easy to misuse them, especially words like "rule over". Yes, it does mean that God has given humans an authority over the rest of creation, but it is not the kind of authority that allows us to grab what we can from creation and forget the consequences. That was never the intention. The words have to be seen in the context in which they were given. God says, 'Let us make man in our own image, in our likeness and let them rule over the fish of the sea and birds of the air' and so on. The 'ruling over' is linked with people being created in God's image, meaning that our 'ruling' is also to be similar to way that God rules.

We know, for example, that God's rule is far from destructive. It is fatherly, loving, just and a great many other things besides. Essentially, his rule over creation has two long term goals: it is always for his glory and it is always for our benefit and the benefit of the rest of creation. Our dominion over creation should be the same – it should be for God's glory and for the benefit of creation as a whole. Anyone who reads this sentence in the Bible and uses it to justify any form of environmental destruction is quite simply guilty of misusing the word of God. So, for example, cutting down a forest for paper, furniture and other wood products is perfectly allowable. God has given us that right and expects us to manage his forests for our good and benefit. But to demonstrate a God-like ruling we should also ensure that we plant more trees to replace those we have cut down ensuring that there are trees for the future. Writing this sentence it seems like common sense, but the state of forests on the earth tell us that this behaviour is far from common. Yes, the amount of forested land in Europe is increasing, but that's only because we Europeans are happily cutting down forests elsewhere in the world and showing a distinct lack of God orientated ruling in doing so! Ruling implies good management or stewardship. It implies thinking ahead and to the future.

Then there is this most difficult of words, **'subdue'** linked to the instruction to '**fill the earth**' (Genesis 1:28). There is no avoiding the fact that this word does mean essentially 'to keep something in control' and it is easy to read into it all sorts of negative connotations. Given the way we use the word today it is very difficult to escape from giving it a destructive meaning. However, we know God would not use this word unless he meant it, therefore there is no doubt that God has given us a responsibility to control the rest of creation. We also know that because of who God is, the subduing he expects us to do can only be entirely positive. Don't forget the wonderful thought that this command was issued before the fall and this very fact means that all five words - rule, work, care, fill and subdue included, must have a positive meaning. Why? Because Eden before the fall was a sinless and perfect place and therefore the subduing that our God expected of Adam must have been sinless too. This subduing must also be done for God's glory and for the benefit of the rest of the creation just as our ruling should be. Perhaps management and development are better contemporary words to use? God has given us the instruction to manage his creation, to keep it under control and use it for his glory and our benefit. There is no way that the word subdue can be used to justify the wanton acts of creation and destruction that are taking place today. Nearer to home, Christians might sometimes joke that weeding their garden involves subduing nature, and whilst this might be partly true, don't forget that the command was given before the thorns and thistles of Genesis 3.18 took hold!

Thirdly, God has clearly given us the responsibility to **"work"** his creation for food and the other gifts created for us to use (Genesis 2:15). Again, this responsibility was given to us before Adam and Eve sinned, so working the land is not something to avoid and moan about, blaming the fall in the process! It is true that after the fall work became harder, but there was work to do before the fall and in fact that is partly why we are here. God wanted someone to look after his creation in his place on earth and he graciously trusted us with that task (Genesis 2:8 and 16). Interestingly, the word 'work' in Hebrew also carries with it the idea of 'service'. Now isn't that just wonderful? In working the earth for our benefit, we are also to think about 'serving' the creation that we work. This principle has huge implications for how we subdue and how we work. Take the forest illustration again. Yes, we can cut down trees for our use, and yes, we should ensure that we manage forests sustainably by planting to replace those cut down. But the way in which we cut down the forests can also show how we can 'serve' God's creation. Cutting down large swathes of trees in one fell swoop for example, perhaps does not display the kind of service that God had in mind when giving this instruction. Not only does large scale tree felling displace the wildlife that depends on the forest but it might also have an effect on water supply and rainfall in the region. I have the privilege of working with Kenyan churches from time to time, and in the west of the country large scale deforestation has affected the previously predictable rainfall pattern, causing major problems for famers. Deforestation can also affect soil quality, allow soil erosion and cause massive problems for communities downstream. I am certain that this is not a biblical way of 'working' the forest.

God quite clearly put things on the earth so that they could be used for our benefit. Eden was a place of abundance and although working the land must have been pleasurable for Adam and Eve, they did still have to work it.

Then we are to **"take care"** of his creation (Genesis 2:15). God cared for his creation and now he is asking us to put his care into practice! The word 'care' is easy to understand. Think again of God as the ultimate caring father of his children, always watching over us, protecting them, doing the best for them, putting their needs first, being sacrificial for them, and you have the right picture. The Hebrew meaning includes these thoughts but also expands them. The words 'care' also means that we are to "serve and guard" God's creation. This is how we should also be caring for God's natural environment and putting this kind of care into practice is both an amazing responsibility and challenging privilege God has entrusted to us. Every parent knows of the trust needed before you give your children over to someone else to look after. Did God maybe feel the same way when he handed his creation over to our care? Imagine, before we bought anything or did anything that might have an impact of the ecology of the creation asking ourselves these questions: 'Does this action show that I care for Gods' creation as he would care? Does this product, this action, demonstrate that I am serving and guarding creation? In buying this product, am I making God's world a better place?' I wonder how much of the stuff we consider buying might get put back on the shelf?

5. Caring for creation – the Rich Young Ruler

The parable to the Rich Young Ruler told in Luke 12:13-21 has a very clear message that Jesus explains right at the start of the story. Someone in the crowd asks Jesus a question, 'Teacher, tell my brother to divide the inheritance with me.' Immediately, Jesus dismisses his question. He is not really interested in inheritance claims. Under Jewish law, perhaps the man had a case against his brother, but Jesus was not on earth to sort out personal legal issues. Instead he uses the question to tell a story related to what might have motivated the question in the first place - the issue of consumption and the attitude we should have towards our wealth and possessions. 'Watch out! Be on your guard against all kinds of greed; a man's life does not consist in the abundance of his possessions,' (Luke 12:15) Jesus concludes

This is an amazing verse. Christ tells us to 'watch out' and 'be on your guard'. he uses the same phrase that he used when talking to the disciples about the 'yeast' of the Pharisees (Matthew 16:6), where he warned them to be careful about how wrong ideas about theology and behaviour could easily infiltrate their thinking. In Luke 12:15 Jesus is saying that greed and the wrong attitude toward our possessions can creep into our minds and take over our thinking. Perhaps it already has! Jesus was warning that wanting more possessions and then trusting that they will bring the happiness we so desire is something we need to be on our guard against. In the Parable of the Sower (Mark 4) Jesus also remarks that wealth is one of the reasons why people fall away, one of the reasons why the seed that falls on stony ground fails to take root (Mark 4:18-19).

But Jesus doesn't stop there. Just in case the disciples were thinking of challenging Jesus by asking about the things we need to live, such as food and shelter, he goes on to tell them to reflect on and learn from how God looks after other parts of his creation (Luke 12:22-31). Jesus points out that if God obviously cares for the birds and the plants how much more will he care for them – and us! We, like the disciples, should not worry about these things. We still have to work for our food and shelter, and have to care for those who don't have enough. But we must have an attitude of mind that trusts God and doesn't worry. It's worth pointing out how remarkable this teaching of Jesus is. Most of us would hesitate before preaching a message like this to say, poorer communities in Africa, and yet in first century Palestine many of the people listening to Jesus would have gone hungry for a large part of the year especially during a drought or when crops failed. We tend to forget that the time when Jesus lived was closers in terms of physical quality of life to poorer countries today than our comfortable European lives, and yet Jesus was telling these people, often on the margins of life, to trust in God for their needs.

Jesus goes on to say that not only is it wrong to put your trust in wealth and possessions, but if God has blessed you with both, then the best thing to do is to sell them and give to the poor (Luke 12:33). Like so many of Jesus messages, these are hugely challenging words and maybe leave us thinking, 'Is Jesus serious here?'

The answer is of course yes he is, which makes it strange that many commentators at this point in their commentary on the passage say something like 'of course, Jesus does not say that it is wrong to be rich', and, 'of course we trust in God for food, clothing and shelter, but this doesn't we mean shouldn't plan for the future' and, 'of course Jesus is not saying that the wealthy *must* sell all their possession and become poor'. All these statements are right and it is good to point them out, but Jesus doesn't say any of these things when talking to his disciples. In making these caveats it is easy to get distracted from what Jesus is actually saying. The whole thrust of this chapter is that Christians should seek the kingdom of God and be on our guard – we should not be greedy or trust in wealth and possessions, but should trust God for our daily needs. If God has blessed us with wealth we should dispose of a large proportion to help the poor and needy.

It seems quite simple, and just in case we should forget these messages, we have an example of how the first Christians put them into practice (Acts 2:45). We also have Paul's instructions to Timothy about wealth in 1 Timothy 5:6-10; 17-19.

However, this is not a book about Christians and the issues of poverty and wealth[14]. The reason why these verses are so important for a book on creation care is that it is largely greed and this desire for more possession that Jesus talks about that is at the heart of the ecological challenges we face today. Putting it bluntly, if we were not so greedy in our rich comfortable country and if we didn't covet our neighbour's possessions so much (Exodus 20:17) then God's precious earth would not be in the mess it is in! Greed is having more than we need to live a God honouring life. If you are older you will remember how much more you have now than thirty years ago. Remember that time when you were just as happy, perhaps more so, and when possibly you were a more energetic Christian? What have all these possessions done for your relationship with God? Have they helped you in your discipleship? Have they helped you to become more holy, more loving towards God and your neighbour? From the perspective of this book, the question is - *What have they done for God's earth?* I'm not going to list them, but all these possessions use the resources that God has provided and produce the waste that God hates. The more we have, the more we damage the earth.

'But I'm not greedy' I hear people say. For many this might well be a true self-assessment. Not every Christian is a greedy Christian. But whatever your reaction, it is worth giving the matter some serious thought. For many others and for society as a whole this is where we come back to my son Tom's diagnosis

of 'delusional necessity' discussed in the introduction to this book. We are very good at persuading ourselves that our greed is in fact not greed at all, but just what God wants for us to live our lives. We are brilliant at convincing ourselves that all the possessions we have and the things we do are necessary. I once had the privilege of visiting the home of a Christian family in India. The family was well off by Indian standards, but their home was simplicity itself. They had the money to clutter it up with all the sorts of things that we have been persuaded that we need, but didn't. When I made this observation they politely smiled and moved the conversation on. The experience was humbling. Here was a family that had chosen simplicity in a country where position and status is certainly judged by what you have.

6. Is our lack of creation care a sin?

If we acknowledge that we are not caring for creation as God expects us to do, then the next step is to ask a fundamental question: When God's creation is damaged as a result of our behaviour, is that behaviour sin? After much reflection I am sorry to say that the answer is clear – 'yes it is'. Sorry, because life is complicated enough for a Christian without a list of new 'ecological' sins to look out for. Sorry, too because I will now have to consider a whole range of things that seriously challenge my own life style.

I am not an expert on the theology of sin but when we think through what God's word says about creation then the only reasonable conclusion we can come to is to see our lack of creation care for what it is - sin. Think of it this way.

- God the Father and the Son created the earth and created it for Jesus.

- We are an intimate part of creation.

- Creation provides us with food, with beauty and a way of communicating God's glory.

- We have been given clear commands on how to live and work in creation.

- We are clearly being greedy - and this is damaging God's creation.

Reflecting on these facts surely there can be no doubt that the damage we are doing to creation is sin. As with any aspect of our Christian life that needs repairing, acknowledging that our lack of creation care is a sin is the necessary first step. Repentance and a changed life should follow swiftly afterwards.

I believe that we need to grasp this nettle and think in this way to motivate us to actually tackle this area of our Christian lives. As long as our greed and the resulting impact on God's creation is something we don't label as "sin", then the temptation is to put it to one side with the result that it appears to be in a behavioural no man's land. This position is simply untenable. Behaving ecologically should be seen in the same way as other expressions of our faith such as loving our neighbour. Indeed, ecological behaviour is part of that love. It is not something that Jesus allows as optional. It is not the case that we should do our best but not worry too much if we fail. We should be worried, seriously worried.

Even if we didn't know before we know now that there are so many aspects of our lifestyles that damage creation. So why are Christians not more concerned? One possible answer lies in the delusional necessity that my son Tom talked about. The argument goes like this: Because many creation damaging behaviours are perceived as unavoidable if we want to live normally in today's society, we convince ourselves that it would be unfair to describe these behaviours (such as driving a car or travelling by plane) as sin. This dilemma is, perhaps, all part and parcel of the challenge God has set us, of living 'in the world'.

7. Are ecological sins different?

The problem is that to some extent we cannot help committing ecological sins. There are so many things that we do each day without thinking that have an impact on God's creation and many of them we can do so little, if anything about. Life in twenty first century society, certainly in richer countries, is designed in such a way that almost everything we do destroys part of God's creation from the moment we wake up. In just switching the light on in the morning in a gas centrally heated house you have made an impact on creation. There appears to be no way out unless we live in some isolated self-sustainable community on an island somewhere. Of course, with these examples there are creation care alternatives, but sometimes putting them into practice is not easy. The problem is further compounded by the fact that as individuals we don't have any control over about half of the impact we have on the earth. This is because wrong decisions have been made on our behalf by governments and businesses that we have very little influence over.

This is what makes being a creation caring Christian so difficult in today's society. It is a struggle to think of examples of other sins that are comparable - sins that are impossible not to commit. Nearly every other sin we commit we can avoid, but so many ecological sins we can't. The question then arises that if it is impossible not to sin then is it fair to label some behaviours as ecological sins? I believe so, but I also believe that God looks at these aspects of our sins in a different way depending on the attitude that we have towards them and our basic position regarding creation care.

It's not just that our decisions and behaviours have a personal impact. They can also affect other people both in our own community and across the world. Very few other sins we commit have this power or global reach. Purchasing something in the supermarket today is just one end of a long chain of decisions, and it is not being over dramatic to say that decisions taken where you live can have ripples across the earth. The frozen shrimps you buy might have been flown half way around the world encased in ice contributing to climate change as they travel. But that's not half of their impact. They also possibly came from shrimp farms created through the destruction of mangrove swamps along a tropical forest coastline. Farming shrimps does not have to be done this way. Mangroves are only destroyed because it is cheaper than the alternatives and we want cheap sea food. The problem is that the destruction of mangroves leaves coastlines more open to the impact of hurricanes and tsunami. Many fewer would have died in the Indian Ocean tsunami of 2004 had not so many natural coastal defences been destroyed. I am not being as trivial as to say that harvesting the prawns in your sandwich caused the deaths in 2004 but it might help focus our minds if we started to think in this way. We cannot claim the benefits of globalisation without taking on some of the responsibilities that these benefits bring[15].

Finally, sometimes we don't even know that we are sinning ecologically. Our impact on the earth is so pervasive and so complex that we don't know the impact that many things or behaviours have on creation. Sometimes this is because we are just not thinking that hard, but sometimes it is because we just don't have access to enough information and sometimes it is a case that we don't even know that we need to know. You might not be aware about the impact of shrimp farming, or how the metals in your smart phone are mined, or how much Chinese factory workers earn. Think of the thousands of products you come into contact with each day. There probably isn't and environmentalist on the planet who could tell you about the impact of every one of them, so what chance does the ordinary Christian have? Finding out about every impact is sometimes such a tough task that there is a strong temptation to just ignore that niggling thought at the back of your mind.

As an encouragement, we constantly have to reflect that that our God is a fair and a just God. He expects us to seek after knowledge and then act on that knowledge, but he does not expect us to act on knowledge that we do not have. He does not judge us for not doing something when we didn't know we should. He doesn't judge the blind in the same way that he judges those that can see (John 9:41). Life today is incredibly complex and much more so than at any other time in human history. Christians two hundred years ago had a huge range of challenges, but caring for creation in the same way we have to was not one of them. People and their physical, social and spiritual needs are the same as at any time in the past, but the political, social and economic situation we live in means that to make the right ecological decisions we need tremendous amounts of information. The same is true of so many other areas of our Christian lives and it would be easy to feel overburdened and slightly panic stricken by how much thinking has to go into discipleship. God doesn't want us to feel like this but he does expect us to work at holiness. This means we are in the odd but necessary situation of having to try and find out more about how we are sinning. To fight our ecological sins God certainly does not want us to isolate ourselves and live in some eco house separate from the world. That's not necessary for ecological sins any more than any other sins. We are in this world to make a difference.

Despite these three reasonable issues surrounding ecological sins the time has come for Christians and the Church to start taking them much more seriously and to drop the excuses. This seems a tough thing to say but since when have Christians been in the business of redefining sin to make life easy? Our job is to restructure society to make life easy and the time has come for Christians to start working harder to redefine creation damaging sins. Creation care is a direct requirement of a belief in creation! If we really believe this then certain behaviours must follow.

8. Dealing with this sin – what is our default position?

So how do we tackle this new sin in our life? Perhaps these last chapters have been a bit of a surprise. Maybe we thought that we were making good progress in our Christian lives then along came another group of things we have to think about.

We all know that some sins are black and white whilst in many other areas of life there are shades of grey. In this respect, the way we obey God's creation care commands can be compared with how we obey God's commands with regard to what we do with our Sundays. The Sabbath is closely related the process of creation. It was the day when God rested and the day he gave us to enjoy him, worship him, learn about him and have fellowship with other Christians (Genesis 2:2-3). In the Ten Commandments we are also clearly told that we should not work on the Sabbath, and other parts of the Old Testament lay down principles for what can and cannot be done on the Sabbath (Exodus 20:8). This is all very clear, but the application of God's command is far from easy.

For example, we know that for a range of people such as doctors and nurses, the police and a whole host of other occupations, working on a Sunday is necessary to save and protect life and hence not a sin for a Christian (Luke 13:10-17). Christians in other occupations should do their very best to make sure that they don't work on a Sunday, or cause other people to work, but the whole way our society is organised makes this an incredibly challenging task. I have already mentioned that just switching on the light on a Sunday morning needs somebody to work in a power station for it to happen. We acknowledge this and although we work our hardest to ensure that we minimise the impact we make on other people's lives we know we will fail.

The important point though is that when we think about working on a Sunday our starting point is that it is a sin. It should be natural for us to think 'should I be doing this on a Sunday?' Putting it in more contemporary language, our 'default position' is not to work on a Sunday, and if we have to work then we should very good reasons for doing so.

In our pursuit of holiness we are always asking ourselves questions about how we should behave as Christians. Should we go and watch that film, should we go to that party, should we do this, that and the other? We ask the questions because we want to honour God. Surely the same should be true of our creation damaging behaviour? Our default position should be not to do anything that damages creation. If we think or know that something we do shows a lack of creation care, then surely we should think long and hard about it. Surely we should be able to justify it biblically to ourselves and before God. The problem is that for our earth damaging sins we don't think in the same way as we do for other aspects of our Christian lives. Far too often we don't think in the first place and our default position is often to do it first and maybe think about it afterwards. Very few people think "If this or that action results in environmental damage then we do need a really good reason to do it". To give a controversial example, it is probably fine for a missionary to take a long haul flight to some faraway place to serve God, but for a Christian to take the same flight to go on holiday should really require a hefty amount of soul-searching.

If we know that something we do damages other parts of God's creation, and do nothing about it when there are perfectly reasonable and easily available options, then we are probably guilty of sinning. If on the other hand there are no reasonable options and the 'something' has to be done, then doing it is up to point probably justifiable. Using our cars to drive older people to church is not a problem, nor are many of the other legitimate things we use our cars for. It could be argued that cars are a necessary part of our society and lifestyles and so it's fine to drive them. This is true, but at the same time we should give thought to the size of the car we drive, whether we could purchase a hybrid or even electric car next time we replace it, how often we use it when we are on our own, do we walk or cycle for very short trips? What is our default position?

As disciples we are responsible to God for the way we live and we are encouraged to throw off all the things that will hinder us in our Christian lives (Hebrews 12:1). We know that on the final judgement day we will have to give an account of ourselves to God. This account will include how we have cared for his creation and how we have shown responsible rule. Surely that is encouragement enough for obedience?

Any sin is serious and ecological sins are no different. It should not be the case that we sit down and ask ourselves how we can reduce our impact here and there a bit. 'Lead us not into temptation' (Matthew 6:13) applies as much to ecological temptations as any other. What other sins could we take a relaxed attitude towards and feel happy about it? If we are prone to anger, make an effort not to be angry at all. We are not satisfied being just a little bit less angry. The same is true of ecological sins. We should want to be good, not just a little less bad.

9. Dealing with our sin - doing our best

Ecological sins then are no different from other sins in God's eyes. Once we have accepted this then we need to start doing things differently through reviewing our current impact on the earth and making necessary changes to our lifestyles. We need to think about our impacts locally and our contribution towards the bigger, more global issues such as climate change. So how do we go about this?

The first step is obviously to guard against any further damage and stop all our creation damaging activities. This will involve reviewing some of the big areas of impact and thinking what we can do to show our care for creation. For a Christian however, just doing no harm is not enough. It is necessary but not sufficient. Biblical creation care should also involve restoration – making things better. As an illustration it might help to compare creation care with the way we care for people. If we come across someone who is damaged in their body or in their mind, we don't just guard them from future harm. We do our best to restore them and to help them get better and back to their original healthy condition. This restoration is what God also expects of us in relation to his creation. We should be working towards restoring it to the condition that it was in before our consuming behaviour did the damage. We should aim to restore Eden!

But God's commands require even more than this. The word 'care' can also mean 'to improve'. In other words, we need to work to make the created world better than it was before we did the damage. It sometimes appears that our ecological behaviour is not so much about a vision of a making the situation better than it was before but just about making sure that things don't get much worse! However, this vision of a 'slightly less bad world' is surely not the vision of a 'restored Eden' that God has a right to expect from those he has given the responsibility of caring for his creation? We shall never reach this goal, any more than we shall defeat sin our lives before Christ returns, but at least we can aim for it!

Imagine you buy a new car and maybe you are terribly pleased that it's a hybrid car or maybe a smaller model than the one you had last time. With the current choices on the market that is not a bad decision, but should we really be so proud? All we are doing is buying something that poisons the earth a little more slowly than the one we had before. We are just being a little less bad, we are not being good! Our lack of a distinctive Christian vision is also why common phrases such as 'carbon neutral' or even 'carbon free' should surely not be good enough for a Christian when it comes to action on climate change? If we are to serve God's creation then we don't just want to stay where we are and not make the situation worse, we should want to be restorative. In the case of carbon this probably means taking stuff out of the atmosphere, not just making sure we don't put in what we see as our fair share. Being a Christian and changing the climate are two incompatible things.

The next few chapters look at these ideas in more detail but it is worth providing a Christian version of the environmentalists 'Three Rs' mantra of reduce, reuse, recycle. For a Christian a better sequence of Rs could be:

- Realise that a lack of creation care is sin, then

- Rethink our lifestyles and work hard to

- Reduce our impact right now, and then,

- Restore creation – make it better

And there is one more important R that should be added to this: Repentance! Once we have realised that we are sinning when we show a lack of creation care and damage God's precious ecology, then surely repentance should be the first thing we do. Repentance for the impact that we have already made and a seeking of forgiveness from God before we move forward and refocus our lives to demonstrate that care that might have been so lacking up until now.

10. Creation care as part of discipleship

Not committing any ecological sins is going to be tough, and restoring creation even harder, but then Jesus did not promise that the Christian life was going to be easy! So what can motivate us to deal with this creation care part of our lives? Taking the answer Jesus gave to the Pharisee's question about the greatest commandment is a good start (Luke 22:37-39). Jesus said, "'Love the Lord your God with all you heart and with all your soul and with all your mind.' This is the first and greatest commandment. And the second is like it: 'Love your neighbour as yourself.'" Loving God and loving our neighbour through our care for creation should be motivation enough.

As Christians we acknowledge that God is Lord of the whole of our lives. Living creation care lifestyles is therefore part of acknowledging Christ's lordship and part of our Christian service to God. It is one of the ways we have of pleasing God and one of the great privileges that Christians have of demonstrating our faith and hope.

Living ecologically involves the "putting to death" all those things that hinder our walk with God and also on setting our hearts on things above (Colossians 3:1-5). It involves not sinning but it is far more than that! It should be exciting, a pleasure and a joy for Christians to be given this fantastic opportunity of caring for God's creation as an expression of presenting our bodies as living sacrifices for Christ (Romans 12:1). This is a unique Christian pleasure that non-Christians cannot share. It should not be a burden. It should be something we praise God for! Ecological behaviour is one aspect of being a good disciple but discipleship doesn't just come about accidentally. It requires hard thinking and hard work! This means that improving our ecological lifestyles is all part of the process of becoming as holy as possible in the sight of God. It is part of the process of sanctification as we tune our lives with how God wants his whole creation to be. Caring for creation is a highly spiritual activity. It's not something we have to do with a sigh and the attitude of, 'Oh well I suppose I'd better care for creation more'. Caring for creation reluctantly and grudgingly is almost like saying, 'Oh well – do I have to pray?' It is an area of our Christian life that we should tackle enthusiastically and with purpose and energy, much as we should other areas of our Christian lives where we know that there are problems.

Chapter 4

God's principles of creation care

1. God's word in nature

Caring for creation is not an optional extra for the enthusiastic few. It is a requirement for all. We know the commands God has given us and we want to live to please him, but what principles has he given us to apply – how do we know what to do?

This book is not a detailed "how to" manual for Christian ecological living. There are plenty of books, web sites and organisations from Christians and non-Christians a like giving useful detailed information about how we can improve our lifestyles. These are referenced at the end of this book. I am going to take a slightly different approach. Over the next few chapters we shall firstly consider the key biblical principles to guide Christian ecological living and then look how these principles might be applied to the biggest creation care areas of our lives.

When thinking of Christian approaches to ecological living it is important to remember that Christians have good news to share! At the end of time, Jesus' victory over sin and death will mean an end to both human suffering and the rest of creation. In the meantime, this victory means that just as we can offer hope to people in terms of their relationship with God and with their neighbours, we can also offer hope to people in terms of their relationship with the rest of creation. We can provide a real motivation for caring for the earth that is not based on selfishness or fear but on a positive desire to obey God.

We have already seen how God's written word has a lot to about how to care for creation. God has clearly told us that we should rule over, subdue, work and care for his natural world. As with other areas of our Christian lives he has also wonderfully provided us with all the guidance needed to apply these principles to our Christian living. We just have to look in the right places and with the right understanding.

2. Some principles from God's written word in the Old Testament – 'Enough for our need'

Many Christians look to the Old Testament for guidance on ecological living and we can find plenty of examples of how God had commanded his people to treat the earth he created and given them as their home. The Old Testament has a great deal to say about creation care, and although some of it can be confusing there are a number of foundational principles we need to adapt our ecological living.

The first is the general principle of consumption. We have already seen from the Ten Commandments that we should not covet our neighbour's goods and how a lack of obedience to this command leads to over consumption. But there is much more to learn from how God deals with his people in Exodus. God was gracious to provide food for the Israelites wandering in the wilderness after leaving Egypt (Exodus 16). They were to collect manna and quails each day, but the provision came with the instruction that 'each one should gather as much as he needs' (Exodus 16:16). This was an important condition and was repeated by Moses a number of times. The condition was emphasised by the fact that if someone collected more than needed it went rotten the following day. I believe that this principle applies to us today. We should consume 'enough for our needs'. This begs the question about how needs are defined and there are no easy answers. Having said that, perhaps even asking the question demonstrates a wrong attitude to the issue.

A second principle can be found in the ordinance of the Sabbath Year (Leviticus 25:1-7) when every seventh year the Israelites were told to rest the land. They were not to sow their fields of prune their vineyards for the year. The Year of Jubilee was another ordinance when every fifty years when land was to be returned to its original owner (Leviticus 25.8-10). In both cases the people of Israel could only eat what is taken directly from the fields and what the land yielded without sowing. Both these have huge social, economic and ecological implications but the key message is one of respect for the soil and the natural world as the basis for life. We should not over exploit our natural world. We should care for it in a way that allows it to continue to produce our food and provide us with water and clean air, year after year after year. For the Israelites this meant resting the land. We live in a different social and economic context and so will have to use other approaches to sustainability, but the principle in the same. Today our God given knowledge of soil science means that land can be used more intensively and although we have abused this and overused the soil, it can still provide more food than Old Testament times without any loss of sustainability.

We need to get our biblical interpretation right when looking at these and other passages and in particular we need to remember that the Old Testament times were a long time ago. When we read the books of the

Law and other books in the Old Testament we should look behind the specifics. We should realise that what we are reading about is how a group of people at a specific time in history were implementing God's principles of creation care. Life in biblical times was very different from life today at least in the richer countries of the world and Old Testament cannot necessarily provide a detailed pattern for living that we should copy. For one thing life was closely linked to the land with most of the population being involved or closely linked with farming. Moreover, the pattern of life was determined by the natural rhythms of the days and seasons. Although both the Old and New Testaments are full of accounts of living in the natural world, it is a difficult to take these descriptions of life in biblical times and draw clear lessons for a twenty first century society and economy.

Much of what we read about ecology in the Bible is found in books of history, poetry and prophecy. These were not written as specific guidance for how we should act in God's creation today. As with all areas of our lives we must be careful about drawing principles for our ecological behaviour from biblical history because there are huge risks of getting things wrong!

127

We should find the principles first and seek God's wisdom about applying these principles in our lives.

3. Some principles from God's written word in the New Testament – 'Love your neighbour'

Examining the answer Jesus gave to the Pharisee's question about the greatest commandment provides a great principle for creation care from the New Testament (Luke 22:37-39). Jesus said, "'Love the Lord your God with all your heart and with all your soul and with all your mind.' This is the first and greatest commandment. And the second is this, 'Love your neighbour as yourself.'" Loving God and loving our neighbours through creation care – what an opportunity for love!

One of the ways in which creation care demonstrates neighbourly love is through improving the quality of their lives. Our ecological sins have negative impacts on other people, not just ourselves. Since moving to the village that has been my home for the last twenty years I have seen local shops close because a new supermarket has opened, new roads built as a result of increased traffic, a natural area taken up by new housing and, most recently, a waste incinerator on the edge of the nearest town. You might see these as positive developments but it so happens that I don't. People and God's creation have been affected by these changes. Of course, these are not all my fault personally, but my consumer behaviour is partly to blame. My demand for cheap food means supermarkets are inevitable, my increased car use means more roads are needed, my production of more waste means it has to be disposed of somehow if it can't be recycled.

It's not just the communities we live in that have been damaged, but as we have already seen, it is also people and communities in other countries. Being a loving neighbour goes even further as we have a responsibility to leave the earth in a good state for those generations yet to be born – neighbours of the future as it were! Trying to do something about our current deluded affluenza-affected lifestyles is one part of the love we can show our neighbour. Love does not just mean offering friendship, helping out, praying for people and so on, but it also means making sure that as Christians our actions do not damage God's creation, and thereby not only dishonour God, but leave a damaged world for our Christian brothers and sisters and our non-Christian neighbours whether they are next door, or far away in another country. You might wonder how to do this? If you bake a cake and take it round to a friend's house this is a fairly tangible (and hopefully tasty) demonstration of love. Ecological neighbourliness is far less obvious and often indirect.

Purchasing food from farmers' markets and local food shops, for example, helps a local economy and ecology in a positive way; taking the bus or cycling means one less car on the road so fewer emissions, again having a local impact. Drinking fair trade and organic tea or coffee directly helps people in other countries, and switching to green energy means less carbon dioxide in the atmosphere which helps everyone on the earth. Yes, your action might only reduce carbon dioxide by one millionth of one per cent, but no matter how small, it is a demonstration of Christian neighbourliness. Then there are the things that demonstrate bad neighbourliness both locally and globally which should be avoided. Purchasing cheap clothes from China is highly likely to have caused ecological damage as cotton uses vast quantities of water, pesticides and fertiliser, and the waste from chemical dyes is rarely disposed of responsibly. Not only that but many cheap clothes are produced using child labour. Purchasing out of season fruit flown from some far distant country has certainly contributed towards climate change. The list could go on.

Ecological lifestyles also provide opportunities for evangelism largely because our new behaviours can be highly visible and give plenty of opportunities for conversations with non-Christian friends and neighbours. People might ask us why we are walking or cycling to church, why we have sold one of our two cars, why we are putting solar panels on our roof, why we are growing vegetables in our garden instead of flowers or doing whatever ecological action we are doing. Not only that, but because ecological behaviour is relatively new it might provide all sorts of new opportunities to talk to people. Maybe your neighbours and colleagues know you're a Christian and you haven't had many opportunities to talk to them about your faith recently. Well here is your big chance! Much ecological behaviour is highly social and the kind of things we talk about a lot along with supermarket prices, what's been on television and sport. Topics like the cost of petrol, how long it takes to get to work, opposition to a new wind turbine and a host of other themes are increasingly the bread and butter of daily conversations. Whether you arrive soaked to the skin after cycling to work during a thunderstorm or you arrive at work on time and your colleagues are all late because of the traffic, there are conversations to be had!

4. Some principles from God's 'creation word' – 'Consider the lilies'

As a well as giving us principles from his written word, God has also shown us how to treat his world through looking at his 'creation word'.

This is not a new idea. Throughout the history of the church we have been encouraged to learn about God from creation. St. Augustine said, 'Some people, in order to discover God, read books. But there is a great book - the very appearance of created things. Look about you! Look below you! Note it. Read it. God, whom you want to discover, never wrote that book with ink. Instead he set before your eyes the things he had made. Can you ask for a louder voice than that?' Luther said much the same when he wrote, 'Now if I believe in God's Son and remember that he became man, all creatures will appear a hundred times more beautiful to me than before. Then I will properly appreciate the sun, the moon, the stars, trees, apples, as I reflect that he is Lord over all things. God writes the gospel, not in the Bible alone, but also on trees, and in the flowers and clouds and stars.' Jonathan Edwards was just as clear, 'We have seen that the Son of God created the world for this very end, to communicate himself in an image of his own excellence.'[16]

Creation tells us about God's power, his wonder, and the fact that he exists. It clearly speaks about him. But creation can tell us more than this. From a practical perspective the natural ecology can guide us in how care for creation. Jesus actively encourages us to learn through nature. In Luke 12:24 he tells us to 'look at the ravens' and how God feeds them and in 12:27 he commands us to 'consider the lilies'. He was talking about God providing for his people by feeding them and clothing them as he did the animals and birds, but we can take his instruction further. The words that Jesus uses when he tells us to look at the natural work around us means more than taking a fleeting glance at the birds and the flowers. Jesus is actually saying something like 'fix your eyes on and take a good look at'. It is possible therefore that the birds and the flowers have a lot more to teach us than we have previously considered.

Perhaps through looking carefully at how God has designed his created natural world to work we might be able to discover deeper principles for Christian ecological living. This is the premise of the rest of this section; that we can learn how to lead creation care lives through learning from nature, from God's created world. Although creation after the fall shows the marks of sin, there is still enough evidence to demonstrate how it worked when perfect! Having said that, God's conversation with Job about his creation clearly warns us that although science has given us tremendous insights into how his earth works, we should not forget that we are not going to understand everything (Job 38-39). There are mysteries Job could not follow and even today we shall only know as much as God chooses to reveal.

The principles that can be drawn from nature can be summarised very simply. Humans have designed a system that extracts materials from nature, uses these resources to make the things we need and then allows us to throw them away when we have finished with them. This is the so called "take, make and waste' system. God designed nature to work in a completely different way which can be summarised as 'borrow, use and return'. There is a wonderful cycle to natural systems and I believe that one of the keys to God-centred ecological living is for us to start taking lessons from nature - taking principles from the way nature works and applying them to our lifestyles.

The problem is that our "take, make and waste" system almost totally disregards the principles God used in his design of creation. There is a wonderful passage in

Isaiah 28:23-29 where the prophet describes the relationship between a farmer and his land in growing grain for food. Twice Isaiah describes how God instructs the farmer in the right way to grow food successfully. In the same way today we can look to how God, in his wisdom, has designed natural systems to work and learn similar lessons to the biblical farmer.

Here are the main principles that we can find through looking at natural systems – as we follow Jesus' instruction and "consider the lilies". It might even help to imagine sitting next to a pond covered in lilies when reading this list. Or, if lilies are not your thing, then just imagine yourself in your favourite place in nature.

- If you look closely at nature you will realise that there is really no waste in a natural lily pond. However hard you look, the things that you might think of as waste, such as fallen leaves, or dead twigs are really food for another part of the system. Putting it another way, all waste is food!

- No part of the lily pond system poisons another part, unless it has a focused purpose in being designed that way. There are no "unforeseen consequences" of toxic materials in nature. Everything has been planned.

- No events take place that reduce or harm the diversity of the lily pond in the long term. In fact, over time, diversity is enhanced. Everything fits together and so supports different parts of the system.

- The whole pond uses only renewable energy (the sun for photosynthesis) and only as much as is needed, not more, nor less.

- The pond system is both fantastically beautiful and effective.

- The lily pond produces an abundance - enough food and shelter for all life in the pond. The key words here are abundance and enough.

- The lily pond is also strong and resilient as a system. It might be damaged from time to time but left alone it will recover.

These are the key ways in which God has designed nature to work. Imagine putting these principles into action in our creation care? What a transformation there would be. For starters, imagine a world in which there was no waste?

5. Aren't these ideas a little strange?

The idea of 'learning from creation' might seem revolutionary to us but it is worth saying that until around three hundred years ago most people lived by these principles without really realising they were following God's way of doing things. These principles are often just normal behaviour for those who live close to the land and depend on it directly for survival. Just consider how food was produced three hundred years ago. It was all local, seasonally grown with organic fertilisers and pesticides and no food was wasted. Whatever was not eaten was used to feed animals. It was grown on a small scale in a way that was in tune with natural systems. Of course there were huge downsides to living three hundred years ago. There was a much higher death rate, people were in poorer health and many suffered from malnutrition, but that does not invalidate the principles. With the better scientific understanding that we have today we can still follow them and be much more productive.

During the eighteenth and nineteenth centuries people began to move away from these ideas largely as a result of the industrial revolution. This revolution was the result of a large number of technological innovations that both separated people from nature and improved the standard of living for nearly everyone. The industrial revolution also resulted in a different way of thinking. People, Christians included, began to see nature as abundant and limitless and with the growth of empirical science they also began to think that nature worked like a predictable machine. In turn this led to the mindset that nature could be used without a great deal of thought because just like the industrial machine; humans could control what happened. If nature broke down then, like a machine, it could be mended. And so the "take, make, waste system" was born. It was this way of thinking combined with the amazing power brought by coal and then oil, changes to the money systems, and the rise of the corporation in the nineteenth century that gave rise to unprecedented levels of creation destruction. It is this destruction that has finally caught up with us. Instead of our technological advances in agriculture and industry supporting the way God's designed natural systems work, they took a completely different direction. Although successful at feeding an ever increasing global population they have resulted in the ecological time-bomb we are currently sitting on. This is an oversimplification, but the move from organising our rule over and care of nature away from God's principles to the human "take, make, waste" system, linked with our delusional greed, is the fundamental cause of the disaster we find ourselves in.

However, all has not been lost! Thankfully a growing number of scientists and ecological thinkers have woken up to the fact that the way we have been doing things over the past three hundred years, despite the unprecedented riches it has brought, has been a long blind alley and that structural changes to our economic systems are needed. In this awakening process, scientists and ecological thinkers have uncovered the principles underlying the way God designed his earth and some innovative business people have even started to put them into practice to demonstrate that they work. Slowly, many of these ideas, often called 'closed loop' thinking, are becoming mainstream. Until now it has mainly been non-Christian thinkers waking up in this way, but there are a growing number of Christians who also believe that the fundamental cause of our current crisis occurred when our economy and society started to move away from how God designed things to work. This should not surprise us. What should be a surprise is that it has taken Christians so long to realise this![17]

One thing needs to be made very clear: In describing God's principles for organising nature it is not suggested that we all have to return to the country and live in a subsistence rural economy. We cannot all be farmers and we don't have to be, but we can still live modern twenty first century lives using nature's principles. Our challenge is therefore to look at how God has designed things, to learn from this and use our God-given wisdom to design new creator focused systems that both supply our needs and give more people on this earth a better quality of life. It is so sad that these principles were not the ones that guided the undoubted improvements of the last three hundred years and that humanist and mechanistic principles were used instead. Now we can rediscover them and we still have a chance to share them with the world around us.

These principles are for all Christians to implement in all parts of our lives. Whatever you do, you can think how to use them. Whether you own your own business, work in an office, teach in a school or work at home as a mother, these principles are for you and should be woven into every aspect of your life. How you put them

140

into practice and the priority you give to the different principles will depend on your own circumstances and the opportunities you have for doing something practical. But the principles can be helpful no matter what you do.

Chapter 5

Consider the Lilies

This section looks at the creation care principles introduced in the previous section one by one. As you read these chapters you might find it helpful to think of your favourite natural place such as a mountain walk, sitting by a lakeside, or working in your garden. If you can read these chapters sitting in this favourite place then so much the better. You will have a powerful illustration to hand as you reflect on God's principles for creation care living[18].

1. We should produce no waste

The most challenging of all principles is to do with waste. It is an overarching principle and one that if we could put it into practice would mean that nearly all our ecological problems would be sorted! If you consider any natural system you will have to look very hard to find any waste and in fact it could be said that natural systems produce no waste at all. Everything you might think of as waste, such as dead leaves or dead animals, for example, are really food for other parts of the system rather than human style waste. God has created all nature to be like that. A natural system is both

142

complex and simple at the same time and this principle of 'all waste is food' is one of the most powerful there is when it comes to our own impact on the earth. Think about it, there are certainly no waste dumps in nature, places overflowing with things that other parts of the system have no use for! Human beings are the only living creatures on earth that have designed our lives to produce waste we have no use for.

Contrast a natural system with all the systems that we have created for ourselves to live in. In the western world we are one of the most highly wasteful societies ever known on earth. At times we go about the wasting process almost gleefully and uncaringly. This is not just about the things that you might throw out each week which actually makes up less than 5% of the waste of the world. I would imagine that most Christians are very careful about obvious examples of waste such as domestic food, water and energy. We realise that waste is not a good thing but it appears that this is one area where belief and action diverge, partly because we use the excuse that there's no alternative or that we are too busy. Concern varies from person to person and generation to generation. My parents-in-law are of a generation that is very careful about not wasting anything in a way that perhaps a younger generation is not.

The real problem is that personal waste is just the tip of a very large waste iceberg. Important though this waste is, it is only one small part of the "take, make and waste" way of making things. We don't actually see around 95% of the waste which is produced in the world, the majority of it created during the manufacturing process. Even before a product reaches your house huge amounts of waste have been produced along the way. Then there are other areas of waste that we don't think about at all such as the gases from cars or the waste produced by the services that we use. Most of the goods we consume have a huge 'ecological rucksacks', meaning that waste is produced making something is heavier than the item being made. That little bit that we see as waste when we worry whether to recycle something or throw it away comes right at the end of long tale of waste woe.

But does this waste matter if it is recycled? Whilst recycling is not a bad idea it's not the best way of dealing with the huge waste issue. This is because the way that recycling works doesn't have a lot in common with God's principles of nature. To begin with you can recycle most products a limited number of times and so recycling only delays the time when an item such as a plastic bottle becomes waste. This is sometimes called "down cycling" and as a short term stop gap whilst we invent a better system it is fine, but it's not a real solution. Secondly, although much of the recycling that takes place is very clever, most of the things that are recycled were never designed with recycling in mind. For example, making items of clothing out of waste plastic might sound like a great idea but in reality it is nothing to be terribly proud about. No one designed plastic bottles with the aim of making clothes out of them when recycled, to say nothing about the wisdom of walking around in a garment made of melted plastic containing toxic chemicals that might have an impact on human health in all sorts of unknown ways! We are almost back to the idea that it's acceptable to sin as long as we clean up the mess. Surely it is far better to design the products properly in the first place so that when they do come to the end of their life, they become food for another part of the system

What God wants us to do is to get rid of waste, as waste - entirely. There is no waste in God's natural systems – so why should we have waste in the systems we have created? Who invented this odd concept of waste anyway? Where did the idea that different parts of

God's valuable creation could be disposed of come from? Why do humans behave so idiotically destroying creation to make a product that we pay good money for, only to bury it in a hole a few years later? Try to imagine what a world might look like if there was no waste at all, or where the waste was designed in such a way as to be food for other parts of the system. This is how God would like us to organise things because that's the way he has done it.

2. We should not poison creation

Think back to the natural area you imagined at the start of the section, but this time look as hard as you can to find any toxic materials there. By and large you will fail! This is not to say that there aren't any poisonous things to be found in nature, but the ones that are there were purposely designed by God to be for their own protection or to get food. In other words, they are meant to be there. God has also designed his world to have healing properties if some animals or the occasional careless humans are caught out. The dock leaves that provide soothing after being stung by a nettle for example! Certainly there are no toxins in nature that indiscriminately poison other plants and animals at random

Now, think how humans have organised things. We are surrounded at nearly every point in our lives by a cocktail of toxic chemicals. In and of themselves chemicals are not a bad thing and our lives would be hugely more challenging without them. However, we use too many of them, we use them too much and we use them in a very unthinking and completely unnecessary ways. Some of these chemicals are used on our behalf to produce the things we buy. Farmers, for example, sometimes come in for criticism because we can see them spraying fields with pesticides and fertilisers. Whilst these chemicals might do a great job in the task they have been designed for, they have many unintended consequences. The significant decline in the European bee population for has been blamed on chemicals in pesticides which not only get rid of the bugs that eat the crops but also kill other insects that do no harm at all.

There are also problems in the use of chemicals on a personal level. Look around your home and in your garden shed and you will probably find enough chemicals to make a lot of people very ill if used in an unthinking way. Although it would take a whole book to list them all it is worth mentioning a few examples. Research has shown that most people use far too much cleaning liquid and sprays in the home. We simply do not need to be that clean, or have our sinks that shiny or have water in our toilets that blue! We don't need to make toys for children out of plastics coated with chemicals. We don't need to put lead in lipstick which is still the case in many countries. Neither do we do need to coat our fruit with chemicals so that it can shine brighter, or last a few days longer. Mothers with babies should be concerned most of all. Many of the toxins in food and other products end up in their most concentrated form in a mother's milk. This is something fed to the most vulnerable in our society We must be more than a little deluded if we think they are having no effect.

I am not against the use of chemicals in principle. Chemicals are natural compounds that occur in nature. I am just against their unthinking and untested use, and their use for lazy reasons. The use of chemicals can become sinful if in using them we break other principles of nature. Chemicals should not be used if we don't know what impact they might have on God's creation or we don't know how they react with other chemicals or if they are used for some pointless purpose. Ray Anderson, the head of one the world's largest carpet manufacturers until his death in 2011, was considered one the leading environmental CEOs. He was motivated to get rid of all but organic chemicals in the carpets his company manufactured by the thought that his grandchildren were rolling around on a product which at the time contained more than fifty different chemicals. None of them had been tested to check that they were safe for babies to lie on. As a result he changed the way he made his carpets and now most of them have no toxic materials in them at all. His factories also put other principles of nature into practice. They produce hardly any waste in the manufacturing process and the carpets themselves are designed to be reused and made into new carpets by the factory once the consumer has finished with them. Interface Flor factories are also powered by solar and other renewable energy[19].

So here is another challenge. Let's make every effort to get rid of any toxic materials in our homes, places of work and ultimately our own bodies. This means both the direct ones we buy to clean our homes and churches, and the indirect ones found in and on the things we buy. Let's clean up God's world.

3. We should not reduce diversity in nature

Continue to imagine your favourite natural environment, home to a fantastic variety of plants and animals - so many that you probably couldn't even imagine the number you are looking at. Our earth is so diverse that even scientists can only guess at the different numbers species there are in the world. Even the soil under your feet has tens of thousands of living creations in each cubic metre.

As you wonder at this diversity, look more closely. Can you see anything that is being purposely destroyed, any species being wiped out completely by other species, any activity that is reducing this wonderful diversity? The answer is quite simply, 'No!' Nature is not designed to go around destroying itself and its own diversity. Over time most ecosystems grow and either maintain or enhance their diversity until what is called a climax population is reached, and then God maintains that ecosystem in balance. Compare this to the way humans have organised our world. We seem to have no worries at all about leading lifestyles that quite consciously set out to reduce diversity. This happens in so many ways. Our desire for cheap food and exotic food results in mangrove forests being uprooted or rainforests cut down. Our desire for cheap holidays has resulted in the mushrooming growth of air networks with the consequent impact on our climate, and the building of tourist resorts in remote places. We have over fished three quarters of the world's fish stocks, some to the point of destruction, and our technological approach to growing food has turned large areas of the world into monoculture plains of one crop. Our climate changing activities also have an indirect impact on species and although some can adapt to new climatic conditions others cannot. This means that a large number of species are guaranteed to disappear over the next one hundred years – around one third according to some scientists. On and on this systematic destruction of God's created diversity goes. Surely this was not what God intended when he gave us the job of caring for his earth? Surely our mandate to 'rule over' and 'care for' does not gives us the right to decide on a course of action that reduces the diversity of creation that God has so finely crafted together. Our task as Christians is therefore to think very carefully about being part of an activity that results in this kind of natural destruction.

Some people might argue that concern for the variety of species is not really so important. They say that the number of species has always been changing, with some disappearing and new ones being discovered (by humans that is, God always knew they were there). This is true, but we should remember that nothing happens by chance. If a species become extinct as part of some natural process then that is fine. That's how God has planned it. On the other hand, if it disappears because of human activity then that's a completely different matter! That's us doing God's job for him without any authority to do so! Sometimes species will disappear from particular places and the balance of diversity can be changed. Fires, storms and floods can wipe out groups of animals and whole ecosystems. This however, is God managed change and doesn't negate the fact that a natural system doesn't set out to destroy itself. Others might argue that if, in following our mandate to subdue the earth, a species or two of spiders disappears then that doesn't really matter. Does it really matter if there is one less species of spider on the earth, especially if it doesn't seem to have any particular use. The response to this is simple. God put the spider there so it must have a purpose, and therefore it doesn't matter if humans find it useful or not. The command was to subdue, and subdue perfectly! God did not say 'fill the earth and destroy as much of it as possible'. We might not know of the use of that spider right now but that doesn't matter. In any case since when has 'useful to humans' been the factor to determine whether a species survives or not? That's a dangerous precedent.

Of course there are challenges with this position and I am not for a moment suggesting that animal and human life should be treated equally. Jesus says quite clearly when talking to his disciples that humans are much more important than animals in God's sight. If it's a case of protecting people from malaria then people have more right to life than a disease carrying mosquito. But the main question is - what is the basis for our decision making? When we are challenged do we have a biblical reason for our action? Our default position should be to do nothing that reduces biodiversity.

4. We should only use renewable energy and only what is needed

Think of your favourite natural place again and ask yourself how is it powered, where does everything get energy from and how much energy is used?

Every ecosystem on earth is powered by solar energy either directly or indirectly. The sun provides all the energy needed for plants to grow and animals gain their energy through eating the plants and each other. This renewable energy food chain works wonderfully. As well as being powered by renewable energy, natural

153

systems never use more energy than they need and certainly don't waste energy. Plants photosynthesise what is needed, and animals don't overconsume.

Now think of our world and compare how we have organised things. Our main source of energy is what ecologists sometimes romantically call 'buried sunshine' or hydrocarbons in the form of coal, gas and oil. We now know that this source of energy has a number of disadvantages. Firstly, oil, coal and gas are finite resources, which means that no matter how much of each of them is left in the earth we know that one day they will run out. We also know that that using hydrocarbons as a source of energy causes climate change. Both these facts are bad news because we depend on these sources of energy to power the lifestyles we are so addicted to. But there is a third problem which makes the situation worse.

The way we use these fuels to generate energy in a form we can use, such as electricity, is incredibly wasteful. For example, around half of the energy in a lump of coal disappears in the energy generation process at a power station. To add to the inefficiency another fifteen percent disappears when the electricity is delivered to our homes. When it gets to our homes it is wasted simply by the fact that most of our houses are over lit, over heated, over equipped and under-insulated. Research has shown that each year most homes gain one or two new lights, that homes are now heated two degrees higher than they were twenty years ago and that the amount of electrical equipment we own has quadrupled. To make matters worse we have deluded ourselves that all this energy is needed, and because of this delusion we actually don't think we are using too much energy!

Hydrocarbons have given us a wonderful standard of living that few would be prepared to give up. The fact that the poorer countries of the world are using the same sources of energy in an attempt to get the same standard of living seems to upset the western world because without a doubt this desire is helping to increase the speed of climate change. But this is hypocrisy on our part. We have to recognise that the way we got rich was the wrong way and that to continue to use hydrocarbons to maintain our current level of consumption is also wrong. Difficult though it might be, we have to start thinking of a world more in tune with God's principles of using only renewable energy and using only what we really need.

Putting this principle into practice on a personal level is difficult because we don't often have much choice over where we get our energy. At a global level the switch to renewable energy is going to be a huge challenge. That is because God has provided enough renewable solar energy to meet the needs of everyone on earth at least five times over. That might seem an amazing statement, but it is true. It is difficult to believe because the current narrative is that that renewable energy is expensive and unreliable. In reality, it isn't. We have just chosen to use other sources of energy for the last one hundred and fifty years. The amount of energy from the sun that hits northern Africa could generate enough electricity to supply the whole of Europe's current needs. The challenge we face is not one of supply or cost, but of political and economic will to invest in renewable energy.

God has been generous enough to provide for more than our energy needs. We just need to put our God-given intelligence into working how best to get at and use the energy that God has given us that doesn't harm his creation and that can be used for the benefit of all. And then work out ways of making sure that we don't use more than our fair share, and don't waste it!

5. We should protect creation's beauty

Some of the thoughts you have when remembering your favourite natural place are bound to be those of wonder and beauty. Beauty as we have seen is one of the characteristics of creation and despite all the damage we have done to creation much of it is still tremendously beautiful. This is true when looking at a whole landscape, as much as on a small scale as we observe a bee go from flower to flower collecting nectar in the garden. Both are beautiful in different ways. It is sad to reflect on the fact that the beauty of creation contrasts so starkly with the ugliness of the world that humans often create.

But what is beauty and how should we seek beauty in our ecological living? The first point to note is that beauty does not just come from what something looks like. We know that this is the way people think, but it is not how God thinks. We humans are very bad at judging what is beautiful because our judgements are infected with sin and very wavering emotions. Our view of beauty is also fickle because it depends very much on culture and time and changes from generation to generation. We often judge other humans by outward appearances but we also do the same with plants and animals. It is much easier for environmental organisations to raise money to protect a large dramatic species such as a polar bear, tiger or panda than an insect or reptile. Our flawed view of beauty that just looks at the outside of nearly everything means that we give money to one and not the other and ignore the fact that all are equally valuable both in the sight of God and from an ecological perspective. The problem is that not all nature fits our current definition of beauty. Even so, despite the fall and despite all that we have done to creation since the fall, all of creation is beautiful and wonderfully made.

Thankfully God views beauty differently. When he looked at his creation it was all very good and all beautiful. Why? Not because of what it looked like, but because it all fitted together perfectly. Everything was wonderfully made and worked as it should and making its contribution to the whole. Despite the fall, this view of beauty has not changed since creation. Looking at a forest or wild natural area, surely it is this 'fitting together' and that makes it beautiful. Individual trees or plants and animals have a beauty of their own, but the whole forest is beautiful because it works so well as a forest. Everything is in balance doing its job. We also know that God does not change and that his view of beauty transcends time and space and so his view of beauty cannot change either. Our view of beauty would benefit from following God's pattern so how do we promote this kind of beauty? God created Adam and Eve and put them in the Garden of Eden to work it and care for it. God declared that his handiwork was very good and it was Adam's job to keep it that way. Adam failed because of sin and we are failing too.

For example, we have the mandate from God to cultivate land for food. Farmland managed according to God's creation principles should be just as wonderful to look at as wilder landscapes. What we don't have is a mandate to destroy the beauty of creation in the process. The large tracts of monoculture grain that upset the structure of the soil and involve the destruction of woodland and hedges to allow bigger fields are hardly following God's plan for the way we grow food. It might be an efficient way of production from a human point of view but it is hardly following God's creation care principles. You might wonder whether we could feed everyone on the earth without such large scale industrial farming, and the answer is 'yes we can.' Plenty of famers throughout the world show that to be true. Feeding the world and maintaining God's principle of beauty are not mutually exclusive.

It's not just the beauty of the natural environment that should reflect God's creation principles. The same should be true of buildings – the places we live and work. I'm not specifically talking about how they look on the outside though this is important. How a building is constructed and how it works are two other things that can make a building beautiful. There are some exciting developments in architecture resulting in some wonderful 'green buildings' that use water efficiently, create their own energy, and have been built with natural materials that truly honour the beauty of creation.

Sometimes we have been so caught up with ourselves that we sacrifice the beauty of God's creation on the altar of delusional necessity. It is high time that Christians reclaimed God's view of beauty and gave more thought to the impact our actions on the beauty of creation. We also need to praise God, that despite all our destructive action, by God's controlling power and grace his creation still displays his glory.

6. We should appreciate that God's world is one of plenty – and one where there is enough for all

Another lesson to learn from looking closely at our favourite natural area is that God has been wonderfully gracious and provided us with a world of plenty. Our God is a generous God. Psalm 104 shows God's provision for his creation[20].

A world of God-given plenty does not imply a world in which we can be greedy and wasteful, though. What it means is that on a global scale God has provided enough of all the things we need for everyone on the earth to be satisfied. There is more than enough of everything to go round. Enough air, enough food, enough water, enough energy, enough of everything needed for a God honouring quality of life. The words "plenty" and "enough" mean that actually there is more than we need, but we don't take it because, if we did, it would be greedy and selfish and some of it would end up being waste. Think of it like eating a meal where you feel just pleasantly full at the end. On the one hand you don't leave the table secretly wanting to go and fill up an empty space with a biscuit, and on the other you are not so full that you can't move from the table. There might still be some food left, but that can be used up tomorrow and you are more than satisfied with what you have eaten. Your eyes were just about the same size as your stomach! That's what God means in his world of plenty and enough.

The message we receive from governments, businesses and even the environmental movement is so different to the message that Christians could and should be sending. Their message is one of 'there's not enough' of everything and therefore, to save the earth (or, more accurately, to save humans) we have to reduce, reduce and reduce again what we consume. What an insult to God! Throughout the Bible we are told that God provides for us fully. If there are shortages then we need to look to ourselves and how we manage things, not blame God's provision.

It is possible to say this despite the obvious fact that there are people on the earth who don't have enough. Each day millions of people go hungry, millions go without water, millions don't have health care and millions don't have enough work, millions don't have access to education, to energy and other basic needs for a fulfilled life. In some cases the word should be billions not millions. The scale of suffering is almost unimaginable but this suffering is not God's fault. At one level, these problems are nothing to do with God. These sinful inequalities are to do with the way that we have organised God's world in way that is wasteful of humans and the rest of creation. If we organise things according to God's principles then we could have a world of plenty for all people on the earth and the whole of creation.

There is only 'not enough' because of the sinful way we use and distribute what we have. It is well known that there is enough food on the earth to feed everyone and that the problem of hunger and malnutrition is largely a result of the immoral way food is distributed. We live in a sad world where people in some countries are worried about obesity and yet still manage to throw away around one third of the food produced, and people in other countries are worried about feeding their children that day. The solution is to make sure that God's 'plenty' is available to all. This might mean some changes in our diets but if this helps people in countries without enough and plenty at the moment it is a change we should be willing to make. Being a vegetarian would help enormously as many more people can be fed from a hectare of land growing vegetables than they can be using the same area to grow food for animals. I am not saying that we must all be vegetarian, but it is a point worth considering in the distribution of God's graciously given resources.

The same point also applies to other things that God has given us. In a previous chapter we thought about energy which we have been led to think is in short supply. This is also simply not the case. It is true that the hydrocarbon based energy we have chosen to build our lives around is running out, but God has still provided more than enough renewable energy from the sun, the wind, the tides and other renewable sources that can supply the world's needs at least five times over, probably won't run out, and have the huge added benefit of not causing climate change. The problem is not a shortage of energy but that we have chosen to use the energy sources that will run out and then needlessly waste them.

God has given us a world of plenty but it true to say that it is also a world of limits. Limits are not a bad thing in terms of creation and in have been put there by God. There is only so much of most things on the earth and although through our God-given human wisdom we have been able to make these things support more and more people, one day we shall come up to limits which our ingenuity cannot push through. If we chose to live creation care lifestyles, then we are a long way off many of those limits but we should certainly not trust to our God-given capacity for innovation to allow us go beyond the limits that he has created. He expects us to exercise wisdom and responsibility in using the plenty he has given us.

In the short term this probably will mean a reduction in consumption and a saving and redistribution of resources, but as Christians we should never forget that the problems we face are a result of our own sin and greed. God has provided plenty and we should be thankful and always challenge the myth that there is 'not enough'. God's natural systems are ones of plenty and enough for all. We need to organise our systems the same way.

7. Natural systems are strong, resilient and effective

Although some ecologists might disagree, many natural systems survive forever after they have reached what is called the climax of their development. Although change is always taking place in any ecosystem as they respond to changes taking place in and around them, they are exceptionally resilient and have an incredible capacity to regenerate. Some ecosystems might appear delicate but the term is only generally used when we are considering the ease with which humans can destroy them. A coral reef ecosystem, for example, is very finely balanced and some might say not particularly robust, but this is only true because it doesn't take much interference from humans to damage and destroy them. Without human interference coral reef ecosystems are as robust as any other system. Fire or wind might destroy part of forest, a long hot summer might dry out plants on a grassland, or a flood might damage pond life, but each of these natural systems has a built in capacity to recover. Most ecosystems are designed by God to be exceptionally strong and can resist most of what is thrown at them and recover.

God's natural systems are also effective in that they are multipurpose systems. Imagine just one fruit tree, such as a cherry tree in blossom and consider what it does! A cherry tree in blossom:

- provides enough wonderfully tasting fruit for food for humans and animals - as long as human aren't too greedy and take them all. We know that the animals will only take what they need.

- produces enough seeds to continue producing more cherry trees.

- gives shelter to birds and other animals.

- holds the soil together through its roots.

- provides nutrients to other plants and the soil through the leaves that fall to the ground.

- filters and cleans the air and water through its leaves and surrounding soil.

- provides beauty especially when the flowers are in blossom.

- is something we can lean against on a spring day and enjoy as we read our favourite book and relax!

A cherry tree is a hugely effective multi-functional part of creation, and that's just one tree. As we look at these systems we should, as the Psalmist did on so many occasions, sit back and wonder - not in the mystical way that so many do, but in a God honouring way. What a wonderful world God has given to us to manage and to manage responsibly. Not to control, dominate or irreparably damage, but to care for and rule over.

How different are the systems that humans have designed! Most natural systems work for the benefit of all plants and animals in the system, whereas our human systems are designed to work for the benefit of a few. The result is that that our human systems are incredibly delicately balanced and are far from being the robust and adaptable structures that many make them out to be. Human systems are almost constantly in danger of collapse and cannot weather the unpredictable changes that often hit them. Our economic system is so fragile and delicately balanced that it only takes a banker to sneeze at the wrong moment and the financial system has the potential to collapse. Other systems we have invented are similarly delicate. In terms of energy supply, it would only take damage to a few major oil pipelines and all the western world's economies would grind to a halt. Our food production systems are constantly being challenged by disease and attacks from different insect species. Our social systems are similarly in danger of collapse. When problems occur we can patch things up and keep the system going, but many end up resembling 'Heath Robinson' like contraptions with bits tacked on here and there to deal with problems as they arise. As a result, most systems have the potential for catastrophic collapse, all because we have ignored God's principles of nature.

In human terms we tend to judge things by how efficient they are. This desire for efficiency is at the root of a whole host of problems, with the result that that our lives are led at an incredibly fast and furious pace, wonderfully efficient at getting things done but maybe not so effective at living as whole. It is this efficiency that often reduces the robustness of a system and leads to the danger to collapse. Let's think of the cherry tree again. A commercial farmer will see the cherry tree as a machine to just produce fruit for human consumption. Hence systems are set up to scare the birds that might eat a few cherries before humans get to them. Fertiliser is added to the soil to produce bigger cherries. The farmer might even grow genetically modified trees which might also be artificially pollinated them to make sure that all the flowers turn into cherries to eat. In other words, a beautiful multipurpose and effective orchard is turned into an efficient cherry producing machine. As a result, the trees are highly efficient at producing cherries but not as effective at being the trees God designed them to be. When an unpredictable event happens, perhaps fewer bees one year to pollinate the trees, or an unexpected storm, then the whole system collapses. Many of our food systems and certainly our soils lack the robustness they originally had and are in danger of collapse as our so called human ingenuity has taken over from God's design.

Ignoring the way God has created things has led us into incredibly unpredictable waters and has resulted in a world far from how God intended it to be. It is time we looked more carefully at restructuring our systems along the lines of God original plan and reclaiming them for him!

8. How all the principles fit together!

The wonderful thing about God's principles of nature is how they all fit together and offer a real hope for the future. A growing number of mainstream scientists are recognising how it is possible to learn from natural systems and they have given this way of thinking a name, the 'closed loop system' or 'cyclical system'. Increasingly, economists and businesses are beginning to take these ideas seriously and more and more systems are organised in this way without us as consumers even knowing about it. The diagram for a cyclical system is shown below.

The waste = food system of making things

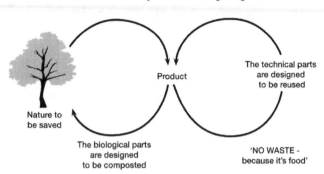

Product

The technical parts
are designed
to be reused

Nature to
be saved

The biological parts
are designed
to be composted

'NO WASTE -
because it's food'

The fundamental principle of this system is that there is no waste – or if there is, it is designed to be 'food' for another part of the same or a different system. If biological ingredients are used in a product then they should be designed to be composted and if technical materials are used such as metals and plastics, then they should be part of a product that is 'designed for disassembly' so that things are used again, maybe in a totally different product or in a reincarnation of the same product.

This is a challenging concept to grasp and best illustrated by an example. What might this system look like for making a common item such as the chairs you have in your church? I wonder what kind of thought went into the decision of the kind of chair purchased? What were the criteria you used? Were they to do with comfort, price, portability and storage, or did creation care come into the decision making process?

Let's assume that your church chair is made of wood, with some comfortable cushion on the seat itself, all held together with a few metal screws and a metal rack underneath to hold song books and Bibles. How should such a chair be made if God's principles are followed?

Firstly, your chair will have been designed very cleverly to follow the seven principles described in this section. The wood will come from sustainable forests and be sourced as locally as possible. When trees are processed there is a large amount of woodchip produced and this will all be used in a micro biomass heat source either in the factory making the chairs, or a local community somewhere. The factory will also use renewable energy for electricity and all the transport, including moving the raw materials to the factory and the finished chairs to the consumer, by using electric vehicles or bio-fuel vehicles. The seat covers will be made from organic cotton, organic stuffing and organic non-toxic dyes. No toxins will be used to treat the wood or anywhere else in the process either. Metals will be sourced carefully to ensure no new metals are mined. Water use in the factory will be minimised and no waste water will pollute local rivers. All the raw materials will be sourced from suppliers that are also following closed loop systems. Workers in every part of the systems will be paid well and have fair conditions of work.

Just as importantly as how this chair is made is how it is purchased. Your church might buy the chairs outright but you might also be given the choice to rent the chairs. If you take the second option, then you can return any broken chairs to the manufacturer who will replace them as part of a rental agreement. The maker will then disassemble the chair and make something else or another chair. If you buy it then the manufacturer will come and take it back from you when you have finished with it and reuse it and reprocess all the ingredients according to a carefully designed plan. The system of leasing products has huge advantages over purchasing them, not least the fact that because you don't 'own' your product, in this case your chair, and labels and fashion become less important. Also, because the product is not 'yours' you are not responsible for disposal. The manufacturer sees the product as a valuable capital resource and so is incredibly motivated not to waste it at all.

This is just a short description of what is really a very complex and cleverly designed process and putting these processes into operation takes time. It took Ray Anderson's company five years hard work before he could make his carpets this way. But as it follows God's principles of ecology it means that it gives us a chance to 'be good' rather than being 'just a little less bad'. It means that nothing is lost from God's natural systems – nothing is wasted, nothing is poisoned.

There is also another huge potential benefit of making things in this way. Because there is no waste and all the ingredients are in a closed loop or cycle, more products can be made from the finite resources we have on the earth. This means more people can be employed which in turn allows more people who don't have enough in life at the moment to have more. By using this system we can stretch the earth's resources to provide a better quality of life for many more people. We are frequently told in the media that if everyone in the world lived the same kind of lifestyles as the average person in Europe then the earth would ecologically collapse. This is true, but only if we continue to live our lives and make products in the way that we always have done. The management maxim 'if you always do what you've always done, you'll always get what you've always got' is very true here. If we change our lifestyle expectations and make things following God's principles from natural systems, then collapse is unlikely. Although people in the affluent west would have to have a little less stuff and different stuff, doing things differently would mean that more resources would be available for those from poorer countries to have a better quality of life.

More businesses are beginning to work in this way and it is up to us as Christians to work out how we can use these principles in our daily lives. To begin with it will be tough because twenty-first century life is not really organised to allow us to honour God's creation. But it will get easier, especially if we lead the way. We should relish the challenges. Being a creation caring Christian is no different to the difficult challenges faced in other areas of our Christian lives in the twenty-first century. We should be used to tough challenges by now![21]

Chapter 6

Putting the principles into practice

1. Change is possible

God calls us to rule, subdue, work and care for his creation. He calls us to do this in a way that follows his principles of creation care – produce no waste, use renewable energy, enhance diversity, make things beautiful, don't poison anything and make sure that everything fits together.

The next step is to put these principles into action. As with many areas of the Christian life the theory is easier than the practice. Suggestions for action that Christians should and should not be doing have been already scattered throughout this book. This section brings them together to give concrete advice about how to live according to God's ecological mandate. In our actions we need to remember that living creation care lives should be so much more than a set of do's and don'ts. Thankfully, in this area as in all others, if we get it wrong we can be confident that God looks at our hearts and motivation.

But before the detail, there are a few general issues to cover. One of the frequently expressed views about personal creation care is, 'What difference can I make? The problems are so huge?' These views are partly right. Our society and economy are so complex that we actually don't have much choice over about half of the impact we have on the earth. Fifty percent of our ecological footprint has been decided for us by the people who supply our energy, design our transport systems and provide our public services. The other fifty percent however we do have control over. We therefore need to do two things: Live more creation caring lives, and influence decision makers to change systems.

So, if someone asks me, 'Is it worth taking action?' I would always answer with a firm and enthusiastic 'Yes'. Firstly, God requires us to care for creation as part of our obedience to him. Whether our ecological living has any impact on the earth is to some extent irrelevant. Obedience is part of discipleship.

The second reason is that history tells us that individuals and the Church can bring about the systems changes that are needed. I have already described the campaign to end slavery in the British Empire in the eighteenth and nineteenth centuries, highlighting the success of an overtly Christian movement in changing society. However, it is also interesting to note that up until the time of Wilberforce the majority of Christians

177

accepted the fact of slavery. Many owned slaves, and some probably invested in slave plantations. A few were involved in trading slaves. Most Christians probably without much thought demonstrated a basic acceptance of an immoral practice. There were probably individuals here and there who challenged the status quo but it is probably true to say that most Christians were deluded into believing that slavery was normal by the same forces that delude us about ecological problems and climate change today.

Then along came the giants of political action such as Wilberforce and Pitt, who worked tirelessly to bring about the end to slavery through the parliamentary and economic processes. 'Ordinary Christians' could do little about the big picture issues other than vote for the right members of parliament (though few actually had the vote in those days, including all women) but they could and did take individual actions that demonstrated support for change. Many families didn't buy sugar from plantations that used slaves. The lesson is that Christians mustn't let the fact that an issue is so big stop us from taking action.

It is true that ecological challenges of today are far more complex than that of slavery and some might argue, less clear-cut. To use the campaigning jargon, ending slavery is a good example of a 'single issue' campaign with a clear and simple goal. Tackling many interrelated ecological issues is a more complicated business, but even having said that, 'What difference can I make?' is not the right question for a Christian to ask. It's not the response we give to other big social and moral issues where we show our concern. Jesus makes it clear that Christians are in the business of changing society and creation care living is one big area that is crying out for change right now. God expects ordinary but extraordinary Christians to live ecological lifestyles, churches to teach about and demonstrate creation care, Christian businesses to use closed loop systems and some Christians to get politically involved.

2. Action One - Buy less stuff

There is no doubt that nearly all Christians in richer countries both consume too much stuff - much of which we have deluded ourselves is necessary - and waste even more! Consuming less and wasting less are therefore just common sense actions we can take. One of the threads running throughout the New Testament is about simple living, starting from the Sermon on the Mount onwards. In reading the New Testament it is difficult to imagine the early Christians being much concerned about gaining earthly wealth and possessions. In fact, it is precisely the reverse that is true. There is plenty of encouragement for simpler living such as the exhortation in Hebrews to get rid of all the things that distract us from running the Christian race (Hebrews 12:1). Although the writer was probably not thinking about being tempted with consumer stuff and the impact of those things on creation that isn't the point. It does give a great reason and motivation to divest ourselves of the stuff we surround ourselves with that we don't really need. Remember too that those in the first church in Jerusalem held all things in common (Acts 2:44). They didn't even seem to own the few things they had.

Consuming and wasting less should be easy to do as most of us clutter our lives with tremendous amounts of unnecessary stuff and waste even more without much thought! In theory there are huge strides we could all make towards creation care and obedient discipleship quite quickly. If only it were that simple! I have already described how clever the Devil is in selling us the idea that that we should judge ourselves and other people by the possessions we have, instead of by who we are. The result of this is that we feel we have to keep on buying and consuming stuff. We are so deluded that it is right to keep on buying more and more that we have reached a situation where our whole global economic system is now based on this continual and growing consumption.

To make sure that we don't fall off the consumerism treadmill the Devil has worked hand in hand with businesses, economists and bankers to develop some very sophisticated ways of encouraging us to buy the things we don't need and then throw them away. If you don't believe this then read what a leading economist said in the 1950's when consumerism as we know it today really took off. 'Our enormously productive economy demands that we make consumption our way of life, that we convert the buying and use of goods into rituals, that we seek our spiritual satisfaction, our ego satisfaction, in consumption. We need things consumed, burned up, worn out, replaced, and discarded at an ever-increasing rate."[22]

One clever method involves the concept of "practical obsolescence." We know that nothing lasts forever. Things break down or wear out so that we need them repaired or eventually replaced and so we have to buy a new one. Buying something new in these circumstances is perfectly acceptable until we realise that perhaps the thing we buy has been purposely designed to last only a short time or to be almost un-repairable. The electronics and white goods manufacturers are current world champions at this. The problem is compounded by the fact that we have got out of the habit of getting something repaired when it breaks down, partly because manufacturers have made sure that repairing is often more expensive than buying a new product, and partly because in some circles repairing something is seen as sign that you can't afford another one. I spent most of my school life with patches on the elbows of my blazer. I realise that school blazers are not so common today, but patches have totally gone out of fashion on any clothing. Even when things have been designed to last a short time business can't sell enough to keep the wheel on economic growth going so another concept was invented – 'perceived obsolescence'. Fashion in other words. It is perceived obsolescence that makes you throw something away even when it works or fits perfectly, simply because you have been deluded into thinking that it is not what is 'in' this year.

Through an all pervading and powerful media and advertising lobby our minds have been captured by these two factors so that we buy stuff without really thinking too much and so contribute to the treadmill of economic growth. If we continue with the same economic system it is going to condemn us to buy even more stuff more quickly and in doing so we are guaranteed to undermine the ecological capacity of God's earth. And there will be nothing we can do about it.

Some of you might be worried that doing with less stuff means a return to living without the things which we accept as being 'normal' in today's world, so let me reassure you. I am not suggesting that we live in caves or a tent, wash our clothes on the river bank, grow beards and eat home grown lentils on a daily basis, or any of the other ridiculous stereotypes that come to mind when simple living is mentioned. Living a simpler lifestyle will mean doing without things but it doesn't mean a return to the past. Christians will still be able to drive cars, go on holiday, use mobile phones and even buy good clothes and many other things that enable us to live comfortably in the modern world. We just need to consume much more carefully and responsibly and be aware that the Devil is truly at work whispering oh so persuasively in our ears that 'it's good to consume', when it patently isn't!

Some people might ask the apparently very reasonable question, 'But surely we need to buy stuff to keep people employed?' Whilst this is true, it is only true only up to a point. This has been the argument used to support all sorts on immoral systems throughout time from slavery to apartheid in South Africa. We are told not to rock the economic boat because people will suffer if we do. For a Christian that response is simply unacceptable. After all, we don't use this argument to justify purchasing a large number of products that are obviously immoral. It wouldn't even cross our minds to use the 'employment' argument to protect these products when they are obviously sinful products to purchase. It would be helpful if we started thinking of more products in this way adding 'creation damage' to the list of criteria we have for not buying something! Creation damage should be as a strong a reason as any other for not purchasing a whole range of products, and employment, or any other argument should not even be on the horizon.

Of course, people will always need to sell things for any economy to function. But if we seek to change our economy to one that follows God's principles then we won't need to buy as much as we do. You might think that this would result in fewer jobs but you would be wrong. Although we might consume less, as our global society becomes richer people in poorer countries will be able to buy more, balancing things out. If the things we buy are made using creation care principles, then everyone wins.

Those who advocate this kind of economic shift are confident that it will create many more jobs across the world, although they will be different jobs and people will be making different things. Building wind turbines is one of the biggest employers in Denmark and the number of creation care jobs is growing daily. Some politicians and economists talk a lot about what they call the green economy, which for a Christian means 'making things using God's principles'. They are confident that this will lead to more people being employed making the right kind of stuff, be this small electric cars, wind turbines, building decent ecologically friendly houses, or growing food that doesn't damage the earth. As an added benefit, these jobs will probably also be more fulfilling.

We are deluded if we think that the stuff that we are being persuaded to buy is always the right stuff. We need to change how things are made and how services are provided so that no ecological damage is done. We should not be afraid of this necessary change and should not be so concerned with protecting the status quo under the delusion that our current way of doing things is the best way. Don't forget that in the business world change is normal. The things we buy are always changing as one technology is replaced by another. We need to make sure that the change is in the right direction and that we embody that change by reducing our consumption and refusing to buy ecologically damaging products. Sinful systems need challenging and our current 'take, make and waste' system is one of them.

3. Action Two - Buy the right stuff

The other half of our impact on creation can be divided more or less evenly amongst five aspects of our lives and it is perfectly possible for all of us to reduce our impact by at least half in these areas if we just did a few simple things. Most of these actions are relatively easy to do as well and are sometimes called 'low hanging fruit' activities - like those easy to pick blackberries right at eye level as you walk down a country lane. Others actions are more like those really difficult to get at large juicy blackberries right at the back of the hedge. You know they will be a challenge to pick and might even cause you some pain, but you also know that it will be worth it in the end. In other words, some of the actions might call for sacrifice, but as sacrifice is a good biblical principle on the road to holiness it should not be a huge problem. Think about it this way: this is one area of our Christian lives where sinning less can really be quite simple.

a. Energy

Our use of energy makes up around one fifth of our ecological footprint. Reducing this impact will involve thinking about where we get our electricity and heating from and how much we use. Most of the homes in Britain use the wrong kind of energy and then allow much of it to leak out like a sieve so creation care action is relatively easy. You don't have to buy a biomass boiler, build a wind turbine in your back garden or invest in solar panels to be more energy efficient. Purchasing energy from a green supplier would be a good first step and there are several companies that guarantee their electricity comes from renewable sources. What might surprise you is that switching providers probably won't cost more. Every Christian should also buy the most energy efficient products, switch things off when not needed and generally use energy as carefully as possible. We should also cut down on the amount of electrical stuff we have in our homes. Given that the average household today gains an average of at least one electrical item a year it is easy to make huge efforts to save energy and find them wiped out through buying one extra appliance or gadget for your home.

Heating and hot water are a little more expensive to get from renewable energy sources and usually requires some financial investment. Hot water can be provided through solar water panels, combined heat and power boilers are more efficient than ordinary boilers and there are domestic boilers that run on bio fuels. Systems those that take heat from the ground are more expensive again. Any spending would pay back in the medium to long term, but until new finance mechanisms are in place the initial investment is possibly beyond reach of many. These new mechanisms are going to come in the near future though. The simplest thing to do is to make sure that your home doesn't leak too much energy by having the best insulation possible in both loft and walls, together with effective double gazing. Turning down your thermostat a degree or so won't kill anyone as most homes are heated around two degrees higher today than they were ten years ago.

In the long term renewable energy is going to have to supply all our energy needs and over the next ten years innovation is going to happen at an ever increasing rate. There will be more opportunities for home electricity generation from solar panels and micro-wind. Hopefully, there will be significant government and business investment in offshore wind, tidal power as well as other technologies such as solar, third generation bio-fuels, and more micro generation systems for homes and communities. Although the technology exists to allow this to happen right now, business is waiting for the systems to be in place before having the confidence to make the necessary investment. So, for the moment most Christian households can reduce the impact of their energy easily by about a quarter and with a little more effort by a lot more. In a few years though, it will be much easier to demonstrate creation care!

b. Travel

Most of us don't think too deeply about how we move from A to B. It is so easy to jump in our car or on a plane. Modern travel is so cheap. We can get to almost anywhere in the world without breaking the bank. What we have to think about is that travel makes up about one quarter of our ecological footprint and that the proportion is growing.

It is good to know that there are some easy things to do to demonstrate creation care. The simplest thing is to travel a lot less, and when we do travel to use buses or trains for longer journeys and cycling and walking for shorter ones. This is all common sense.

There is no getting round it. The car has improved the quality of life for most people. We have so much more mobility now than we did in the past which makes life more convenient and fun. For many people a car is an essential part of life for work, getting to church, and so on. Life is unimaginable without them despite the downsides such as traffic congestion, noise, air pollution the possibility of an accident. Much as I would love to say 'don't use a car,' I can't. However, making an effort to use our cars less is essential and most of us could manage fewer miles in our cars if we really tried. The problem is that we hop into our four wheeled friends without thinking about the alternatives. Anything up to a mile and it is often simpler to walk. For distances of up to five miles it is often quicker by bike. Once you get into the habit like the Dutch or the Danes, cycling is almost easier than using a car.

However, it is tough sometimes. If car use is essential, then thinking about the kind of car you drive is the first step to improvement. Making your next car a smaller car or hybrid is a start, and an electric car would be even better if you do a lot of short journeys. These are still quite costly, but leasing them is often a realistic option and in some larger cities there are short term car hire schemes that are successful if you are only an occasional car user.

Some of these options will mean rearranging your lifestyle here and there, but who said not sinning was going to be easy all the time! We are willing to fight sin in other areas of our lives through sacrifice, so why not creation care as well?

The biggest impact that many Christians have relates to the tricky issue of air travel. One flight, especially a long haul one, will cancel out every effort you have made to reduce your carbon dioxide impact on creation in every other area of your life. All the efforts made to reduce your ecological footprint through purchasing renewable electricity, having home insulation, walking and cycling more, buying less stuff and the right stuff could go up in smoke through taking one long distance flight. Thinking of it that way might help. A return flight to Thailand produces around 3000 kg of carbon dioxide. That's as much as an average produces in three years driving a small car. Some might ask whether planting a tree every time you fly to absorb the CO2 produced by a long haul flight is a possible solution. I'm afraid that the answer to that one is no, not really. For a non-Christian it might work, but for a Christian this kind of idea is a little bit like paying someone else to sin for you. This is not something anyone would think of doing in other areas of life. Imagine saying 'I'm too busy to pray and read God's word today so I'll pay someone to do it for me.'[23]

Some Christians, such as missionaries, have to travel. Others might have to travel for their work or visit their family living in another country. In these cases it would be worth thinking how your brothers and sisters in your church could reduce their carbon emissions by the same amount that the flights generate. We sacrifice our money to support mission work and could sacrifice our carbon emissions as well. Flying to go on holiday is another matter entirely and difficult for a Christian to justify. Holidays in places far away can be truly amazing but they are hugely damaging to creation. Fifty years ago hardly anyone flew on holiday and can we honestly say that people were any the less happy or holy then?

If you really want a chance to talk to your neighbours about your faith and ecology and what motivates your behaviour, then travel is one sure fire way of stimulating conversations. Telling your neighbours, friends and family that you have stopped flying is sure to excite interest. How about buying a bicycle if you don't have one (and using it), knowing the local bus timetable (and using it), making your next car (if there is a next one) an electric car, parking it proudly on your driveway, and travelling by bus and train on your next holiday?

c. Food

The food we eat makes up about a quarter of our ecological footprint. Two hundred years ago it took around one and bit calories of energy to produce a calorie of food energy. Now it takes around ten calories of energy to produce one calorie of food. These calories are spent in the making the fertilisers and pesticides used on crops, the machinery used to plant and harvest what we eat, the cost of processing and packaging and of course all the transport involved. This is unsustainable and more than a little stupid in an age of the reducing availability of hydrocarbon energy and growing world population. It just doesn't make sense to spend ten units of the world's energy to make one unit of energy for human consumption. There is also the fact that the way food is produced is hugely destructive of biodiversity and soil structure. We know that vast areas of rainforest are destroyed each year to grow soya to feed cattle and poultry, but even nearer home the impact on wildlife of our over use of pesticides is becoming obvious. The declining bee population has already been noted.

Changing what we eat and how we eat probably does mean making an effort as shopping for food is a complex activity. Most of us do a weekly shop in a supermarket and buy a large number of different products at a time, each one with a different impact on the earth. It is not so easy to care for creation here, partly because of the level of decision making required and partly because as yet there are very few one stop shop alternatives for ecologically acceptable food. It is likely that things will change quickly over the next few years. There are already local and organic supermarket chains in some European countries, and hopefully their time will come here in the not too distant future.

There are a number of good ways of cutting the size of your food footprint relatively simply. Whilst recognising that eating meat is not wrong, the easiest way of reducing your impact is to become a vegetarian or at least cut your meat consumption significantly. It is well known that you can feed far more people on a vegetarian diet from one hectare of land than you can feed meat eaters. With at least a third of the world going to bed hungry each night linked with a growing population linked with a finite amount of farm land, greater levels of vegetarianism should be a serious option for the future.

If this does not appeal to you then the next most important contribution you can make is to buy as much local and unprocessed food as possible. Local food is important because by definition it has not travelled far and hence has not generated a lot of carbon dioxide through transport. Farmers markets guarantee relatively local produce and more shops also sell local food. Buying less processed food is important because vast amounts of energy are spent in transforming food in different ways. Buying less processed food means careful shopping and doing your best to avoid all the stuff in breadcrumbs, sauces, ready meals, frozen foods and so on. Buying fresh food and only food that is in season is also good. Another contribution would be to purchase organic food where possible. If you really want to push the boat out in terms of ecological living, then join the increasing number of people who are growing their own food. Those who know me know that I am no gardener, but the possibility of intercropping the flowers in our garden with vegetables next year is a very real one!

Not wasting food is another positive action. Again, it's already been said that at least 35% of food in Europe is wasted through food processing and by supermarkets. Many vegetable farmers have to grow more than they know they can sell because they know that some of their product will be not accepted by the supermarkets because it is the wrong shape or size. The farmer's contract with the supermarket often might mean that they cannot sell these perfectly edible but misshapen vegetables elsewhere. Supermarkets also throw away vast quantities of food that is just out of date. Buying unprocessed food and food from smaller local suppliers also reduces this food waste.

d. Other goods and services

The final part of our footprint is made up of everything else we buy, such as clothes, furniture and electrical goods, and a large number of services that we use - schools, hospitals, cinemas, theatres and sports grounds. Currently only very few of these items do not leave any mark on creation and we buy such a large variety of goods and services that it is difficult to make concrete suggestions. Buying fewer of these has already been mentioned as by far the easiest way of reducing your footprint, followed by keeping the goods we buy for as long as possible and mending them when they break down. If you want to be radical, then there are also an increasing number of sharing and swapping schemes to enable you to get rid of something you no longer have a use for and know that it is going to good home.

All the same, we all need new things now and then and so it's good to become an ecologically inquisitive consumer. We are generally happy to ask shop assistants about the price of things, so all we have to do is develop a new line of questioning about ecological impact of the things we buy to find out how closely a product has been made following God's principles of ecological design. With a little research we can make sure that we choose things that damage the earth less. There are an increasing number of companies selling organic and fairly traded clothes, and there is also a greater choice of electrical goods that consume less energy and are designed in a way to be reused when you have finished with them. Electronic goods are still a big challenge, especially mobile phones and computers. These have rare metals in them such gold, which is often mined in a very ecologically destructive way, and often contain coltan which most probably came from the Democratic Republic of Congo where the metal is mined by enforced child labour and where the income is used to support rebel groups. Phones and computers are highly damaging but real ecological alternatives just don't exist so, assuming that life cannot be lived without them the best strategy is to keep them as long possible.

The services we use are also improving step by step and hotels in particular are taking part in some form of eco labelling scheme. This doesn't guarantee ecological perfection but at least people are trying and moving in the right direction. Whatever we buy the key question to ask is - do we really need it? We need to become thinking consumers. If you have a choice, make a creation care decision.

e. Money

There is a fifth thing that isn't part of our ecological footprint but which also requires our attention. Quite a number of Christians could review how the money we have invested is used. If you do have money saved, do you know what your bank or building society does with the money in your name? Maybe you do, but it is worth finding out simply because your money could be invested on your behalf in all sorts of creation destroying activities and with companies that don't have many concerns about how they treat God's world. It's a little pointless you switching your energy supplier and cycling everywhere thinking 'Wow, that's great –

I'm honouring God!' if the money you have invested is going to fund the development of an ecologically destructive oil field, or a factory in a country where the workers are paid less than a living wage. It is worth thinking about switching money to a bank or fund that has a policy about the ethical use of your money and there are Christian advisors around who can help you with this. You might earn a little less with ethical investments than earth destroying ones, though this is not always the case.

Finally, there is a critical thing that all Christians should be doing before making any decisions: prayer. Prayer for personal wisdom and strength, prayer for churches, prayer for national and global decision makers, prayer for those who are affected by our ecological sins, prayer that those businesses that encourage this sinning will change their ways and prayer for forgiveness for past ecological sins! Constant prayer!

Many of the actions suggested are not going to take you too much time or energy or money. Changing won't make your life even a little bit less worth living either. In fact, the changes you make will probably make your life better and certainly a lot healthier, both physically and spiritually. But even if they do take a lot of effort is that the point? Surely each of us should have some plan of action that will help us to become better disciples by reducing our impact on God's creation year on year.

4. What should organisations be doing?

a. How about your church?

Churches need be involved in creation care both by leading by example and teaching church members how to align their lives more with God's will for creation care living. The Church is the body of Christ and because caring for God's creation is such an important part of Christian living then surely if the Church does not live ecologically the body itself is damaged. Making sure that our churches both act and teach God-centred ecological living is therefore a key thing for us to do.

God's principles of nature and the five areas listed in the previous chapter apply to church life as well as to individual Christians. The ideas below are not exhaustive but are meant to be a starting point to provoke thinking and discussion at church meetings.

- Energy – electricity and heating. Where does your church building get energy and light from? What are the sources of energy? Would some solar panels (for hot water or electricity) provide opportunities for witness as well as reducing electricity bills? If your church has a chance, what about a wind turbine, a combined heat and power boiler – there are so many opportunities!

- Travel - how are people attending church encouraged to travel to church? Do members of the congregation car share? Is it possible to cycle or walk to church? Does the church have secure cycle racks protected from the rain for those that do cycle? If your church has a minibus what kind of fuel does it use? The issue of using public transport on a Sunday might be a controversial one for some people, but if it is the only way for some to get to church then are services timed to allow the most people to attend?

- Food - What kind of food and drink does your church serve? It is to our shame that most cafes and restaurants are way ahead of many churches in terms of the use of fair trade coffee and tea and organic milk? How is it served, in plastic disposal cups or something more sustainable?

- Other things that churches consume and buy such as furniture, multi-media projectors, books and so on and so forth. How much creation care thinking has gone into their purchase?

- And finally, your church probably has a bank account. Do you know how the bank uses God's money? Does your church bank have an ethical or ecological and climate change policy? Is it worth asking next time you bank the Sunday collection?

If your church doesn't do much in terms of action or teaching on these topics then there are plenty of places to start. If you are a church leader it might be useful to reflect on the last time there was any serious teaching about creation care rather than perhaps a few application examples at the end of a sermon on evolution or at a harvest festival. You might also think about how often ecological issues are raised in the prayer meeting, or whether climate change ever been the subject of a Bible study. Taking creation care seriously is not a replacement for teaching the good news about salvation, nor should it deflect the church from that task, but it should be seen as an essential part of holy living. It deserves more attention than it has generally been given in the spiritual life of the church. We should never forget that ecological living is a spiritual activity!

Individuals and churches have to make their own decisions about how far to get involved with Christian and non-Christian environmental initiatives. In common with social initiatives many Christian ecological organisations are incredibly broadly based and some might feel uncomfortable about sharing activities with groups who have a different statement of faith or none. Others might consider that in the early days of any social movement then broadly based organisations are acceptable if it means that there is at least some form of Christian witness. Both positions, as well as those in between, are fine. However, if aligning your church with part of a bigger movement is not possible, then at least do something as an individual church. Start something that you would feel happy being part of, rather than sitting back and bemoaning the lack of a distinctive group.

b. What should other Christian organisations and businesses be doing?

It is not only as individuals or families and in Churches that Christians need to take action to demonstrate creation care. Christian organisations should also be publically demonstrating that through the way they work they take God's creation seriously. This will mean going through the five areas outlined in the previous chapters in relation to the mission of the organisation or business and making sure that the way the organisation operates matches up to God's requirements.

In general terms, for Christian organisations and businesses this might mean having a policy on transport to encourage people out of their cars and onto public transport, considering energy use in offices or the use of computers and other electric goods, and purchasing green energy. There might be a need to review investment policy and the purchasing of other consumer goods.

More specifically, organisations and businesses will need to look carefully at what they do and ask themselves what God requires. A Christian publisher might need to focus on issues such as the origin of paper used, the use of newer technologies such as print on demand and the use of the internet. A Christian evangelistic or training organisation might need to look more carefully at transport around the country. A Christian conference organiser will need to look at how people get to and from events, how event food is produced and the nature of the accommodation. Many non-Christian organisations from coffee shops through to fashion retailers have sections on their web sites saying how they care for the environment but very few Christian ones seem to do the same.

Businesses run by Christians also have tremendous opportunities and responsibilities, especially those that might be involved in the manufacturing process. Following a cradle to cradle or closed loop model of making anything is a huge challenge, but there are people out there doing it and who can help. It would be wonderful if in five years time the top ten beacon businesses in terms of ecological processes and products were all run by Christians as a demonstration of their faith and God's grace! This is not just about making so called 'green products' but it's about making everything a green product so that things designed according to God's principles of nature become normal!

5. Doing the right thing in the right way

Refocusing our lives to show a greater level of creation care will be a challenge. It will take some hard work and hard prayer but be delighted by every small step you make and also take encouragement from the fact that more and more Christians each day are thinking the same way as you. There are a growing number of people and churches that are putting these principles into practise and we need to seek these out and share the examples of good things that are happening. There is a lot of good news and the web sites listed at the end of this book will keep you in touch.

Living a creation care life is a challenge and when we have made a change there is a temptation to think that everyone else should do the same. Every Christian will start from a different point and every Christian will have different resources and different opportunities to make changes. Whilst there are basic biblical principles to follow for ecological living, no one is going to be able to make all the changes in their lives overnight and ecological perfection is not going to be possible in this world. For that we shall have to wait until the next! It is up to individual Christians to come up with their own plan of action and put this into practice. We are responsible to God for our ecological living. We need to lovingly acknowledge our differences and pray and support each other in our ecological goals, confident in our own minds that we are doing all to the glory of God (1 Corinthians 10:29-31).

Chapter 7

So if we do all this – will it save the earth?

1. God is in control

Christians should be living more simply through consuming less and consuming things made in the right way. These are also the two major approaches taken by the environmental movement, business and politicians, though of course motivated by a different set of reasons. Christians care for creation because first and foremost we want to honour God. Those who are not Christians care for other reasons, but even with our radically different foundations for thinking, it is worth asking the question, 'Will these actions work?' Will we be able to 'save the earth'?

Before answering that question it is important to restate that despite all the ecological problems humans have caused, it is God who is in control of the earth and it is God who holds all things together. At one level it is not our job to 'save the earth' ecologically. It is our responsibility to live Godly lives and encourage others to turn to him. In this way our attitude to creation care can be compared with our thinking about evangelism.

Sometimes we fall into the trap of thinking that it is our evangelistic activity that brings people to Christ. We forget God's sovereign purpose. So it is with our ecological behaviour. Our desire to live more creation-caring lives should not be because we believe that it is our job to save the earth, it should be because we want to obey God. This obedience should be a pleasure and joy, not a burden! God demands obedience and faithfulness and whether that brings success in human terms is not the main issue.

So, will living simpler less consuming lives and buying the right stuff 'work'? The simple answer is that they will. It is possible to live a simpler lifestyle, having all the things that are needed for a satisfying life, without destroying the earth. All the things that are really important, such as good education, health care, shelter, mobility, rest and recreation, are all possible. They are also possible not just those living in richer countries but also for those especially in poorer countries who currently don't have enough. Before you breathe a sigh of relief, there is one huge "but". Consuming less and consuming 'right' will only work if everyone manages to put them into practice. As we know from other areas of our Christian lives, our sinful nature means that this is unlikely to happen. Encouraging people to behave in a way that honours God, but without a faith in God to motivate new behaviour patterns is almost an impossible task. If we could manage it, then wars, poverty and hunger would all end tomorrow. I have to be honest, the motivation for writing this book is that even many Christians don't live creation care lifestyles, let alone those who don't believe! There are a number of groups of problems we face in getting the change that is needed. They are all linked and all are to do with an understanding of human nature.

2. Living a simple lifestyle is not attractive

Working towards a simpler lifestyle is not uniquely a Christian goal. The idea of 'voluntary simplicity' has always had its followers. Leading less consuming lifestyles is one of the most important strategies to encourage environmental behaviour adopted by government, business and the environmental movement. It can be seen in the multitude of 'do your bit' campaigns and all the exhortations to "save" this that and the other, together with the 'if everyone did this' approach. For those who are not Christians the simplicity approach has two fundamental flaws.

Firstly, it relies on perceived sacrificial personal behaviour change. Although the environmental

210

movement talks about raising awareness and changing values and attitudes what is really meant is changing people. As Christians know all too well, human beings are essentially selfish and me-focused to the core. Although you might think that changing behaviour to protect the earth for current and future generations might be attractive, the research evidence, as well as the evidence of our own eyes, clearly says otherwise. The reason is not difficult to understand. If people equate success with having more and more, then the logic is that is that having less is failure. Because humans are so addicted to the me and success way in which society functions, relying on people adopting simpler less consuming lives is almost doomed to failure from the start.

A second weakness is that if voluntary simplicity is to work, then everyone has to do it. If only a small proportion of the population live simple lifestyles then not much will change. Most people will carry on consuming leaving the simple lifestyle people to enjoy living simply! There might be one or two people willing to reduce the scale of their consumption for the sake of humanity as a whole, but not the majority. The idea that everyone will voluntarily consume less shows a remarkably poor understanding of human nature and behaviour! Although voluntary simplicity seems such a reasonable concept, its weakness lies in the fact that enough people have to be motivated enough to live these simple lifestyles and for those who are not Christians little motivation exists.

To some extent the environmental movement has recognised this and most campaigns try to encourage simple lifestyles for a range of 'me' focused reasons. They suggest that we must protect the environment to ensure that we have food security, to make sure we don't destroy the plants that could be used to treat cancer, and to avoid extreme weather events and flooding. We must make sure that the earth is habitable for our grandchildren. If these reasons usually don't persuade us to stop damaging creation then we are encouraged to 'save the earth' because it will save us money! What a sad reflection on twenty first century society. Despite our materialism it's been demonstrated that the saving money concept doesn't work all that well either unless a lot of money is involved, and ironically if money is saved then often people spend it on more consumer goods, undoing all the good they have done.

For Christians, voluntary simplicity is all about pleasing God. This is a tremendously powerful motivation that only those who know God can understand. We want to care for creation to show our love of God and our obedience to him.

3. People are confused – Greenwash

Many people are also confused about what to do. On the one hand we are being sold a simplicity message, whilst at the same time being encouraged to carry on consuming to save the economy! This is why many ecological change campaigns are usually dressed up with a suitable gloss to appeal to our inner greed and selfishness. 'I want to help and do my bit and I'm willing to change as long as I don't have to give up too much'. It is also why there are so many green products out there to appeal to our desire to shop. The problem is that many of the so called green solutions to sustainability are at best a green gloss and at worst a green deception.

Look around at many of the environmental products and behaviours that are being sold. Ask yourself how far they go towards putting God's principles of nature into practice and you will find that very few of them come anywhere close. Almost anything that you purchase is by definition damaging the earth, no matter how green it claims to be. The green credentials of a product are often nonsense when you look at the whole impact or life cycle of a product. Organic cosmetics are a good example. The product inside the tube might indeed be ecological, but when you think about the packaging, the transport of the product and how it was actually made, then the green shine begins to wear off. What the manufacturers really mean is that their green products are a little bit better than non-green ones on the market. They encourage us to purchase things that are a little less bad for the earth. They are certainly not as ecological as God would like them to be. They are certainly not "good".

Green marketing is also exceptionally clever at deluding and confusing us to buy green products even when the ones we have already work perfectly well. In life cycle terms there is no way that a new green product is necessarily any better than your old product, especially if the old one works perfectly well. Green marketing is great at convincing us to buy things we don't even need, but we feel it is fine because it's green. The result is that we clutter up our lives with a mass of unwanted but green goods! The basic principle is that if you don't need it, then it's not green. It's as simple as that. Unless the stuff you buy has been made following God's principles of nature then it cannot be really green and it must have damaged creation somewhere along the way.

We should admit that we have been taken in, deluded by the possibilities of green consumption. When offered the opportunity to have our cake and eat it, we grasp it with both hands. As some people have noted, we haven't just been brainwashed, but 'greenwashed' as well!

4. The system is broken

Green deception and green delusion is making people seriously confused, but it's only the thin end of the wedge when compared with how political and economic decision makers behave. Politicians often claim that society is broken. What they and business need to understand is that God's creation is broken too. This judgement sounds harsh and you might think unfair, after all, there are plenty of wonderful initiatives that help us to live more creation care lifestyles? Many have already been mentioned: we can buy fair trade and organic food, we have farmer's markets, we have better public transport, there are more cycle paths, we can install solar panels and buy green energy. There are one hundred and one things we can do. This is all true and all necessary. At the same time, even all of this is not sufficient. The problem is that much of the action falls far short of what is needed.

Many of the creation care initiatives tackle the symptoms of the problem rather than the root causes and in doing so often place a reliance on technology and market mechanisms to solve the problems. For example, although many of the solutions to climate change focus on technologies to reduce carbon dioxide in the first place, others concentrate on what to do with it once it has been produced. In the case of power stations, the idea is to capture carbon dioxide and bury it underground rather than producing less in the first place. Financial mechanisms include carbon trading schemes and carbon taxes to discourage producing too much carbon dioxide, rather than simply passing legislation to reduce CO2. The problem with these initiatives is that they accept the continued production of vast amounts of carbon dioxide rather than challenging the need to continue to emit climate changing gases.

A second weakness is that current green policies appear to lack an appreciation of the huge scale of the challenge. It has already been noted that whatever we do, the average global temperature will be two degrees Celsius higher in 2050 than it is now. To make sure it doesn't rise even more we have to reduce carbon dioxide emissions by between 80% or 90%. There are other scary statistics relating to the declining quality of soils across the world – that thin layer of earth that provides our food; declining water sources; declining fish stocks and declining biodiversity. Each one of them is a huge challenge. Taken together they represent a crisis of enormous proportions.

Few world leaders seem prepared to face up to the scale of the changes needed. Two examples will suffice. No country in Europe looks like achieving the promised reductions in carbon dioxide emissions. Despite the ambitious targets set at national and international levels the necessary policies and investment needed to reach the targets are simply not in place. European countries have also failed to meet their targets for biodiversity conservation. Few leaders realise that time is running out. Current green policies have failed in their lack of vision though it is to be hoped that this will change in the future. Governments need to do much more!

A third weakness relates to a theme that has been a thread through this book. The fundamental problem is the flawed way we live in God's creation and the way we challenge the ecological limits God has graciously provided. The whole "take, make and waste" system is essentially broken, yet most of the economic and technological green "solutions" don't recognise this. They assume that the system itself is basically sound and that what is needed are a few changes here and there. It is agreed that some of these changes will need to be major ones, but the nature of the system itself is rarely challenged. It is difficult to get decision makers to see that constant economic growth and a "take, make and waste" system of production are simply not possible on a finite earth. A slightly improved flawed system is still a flawed system. What is needed is a new system!

There is a serious lack of political will power, economic understanding and dynamic leadership needed to make the changes happen. Despite what is being claimed, if politicians and businesses really wanted to 'be good' then they would be making much bigger efforts than they are. Their behaviour is, of course, partly our fault because our national and international leaders want give us messages that they think we like to hear. One of these is that being green will not take too much effort, energy or money. The problem is that this is simply not true! The switch to a more ecological society is going to be a hard one, and whilst this is a depressing message to read, take heart, the final chapter has more to say about God's way forward.

5. So is there any hope?

Whether the earth as it is today will be around in fifty or one hundred year's time is a matter for God alone. We don't know when Christ will come again and when the new heavens and new earth will appear. Should God choose not to return soon there are reasons to be optimistic about the future of the earth.

If everyone on earth became a Christian and lived creation care lifestyles, then it would be good to think that the problem would be solved. Indeed, if everyone was a Christian then other challenges such as poverty, hunger, injustice and war would fade away. We would all love that to happen, and bringing the message of salvation to people is obviously the most important responsibility we have before us. However, until that day comes, or Christ comes again, we have to put other solutions into practice. If simple living and the current global green policies won't work, what will?

The answer lies in nothing short of a revolution and lies in putting God's principles of nature and for ecological living into practice in every area of our lives. The scale of the problem means that slight shifts in thinking and behaviour won't work. There has to be a fundamental change in the way all businesses make the things we consume, the way our economic system is structured, and the attitudes and values people have towards both other people and the stuff we buy. If a such a one hundred and eighty degree turn can be managed then the earth will be restored, and although it will never resemble the perfection of the Garden of Eden, it will be an earth that can properly glorify the Creator!

It is a huge challenge, but thankfully there is evidence and experience around to suggest that it can be done, both in terms of the technology and systems needed and the changes required in people's values and attitudes. Previous chapters have given examples of businesses and systems that exist right now that follow God's principles of nature in the way they operate. More of them are needed. More Christian activity is also needed. More thinking Christians, more churches taking creation care seriously, more Christians in politics and business putting God's nature principles into practice.

Although complete changes in the way things are made and a new economic system will essentially solve the fundamental ecological and climate change challenges, much more is needed to bring about a truly sustainable

220

and fair world. It will take new values and an entirely different framework of thinking. Although changes in this area are much harder than technical and economic changes, it can be done with the right level of Christian commitment and the right approaches to engagement. There are plenty of examples from history of Christian values being put into practice in society, although not always by Christians themselves.

Bringing about new economic and technological systems is going to involve change but this is nothing to be afraid of. Change is a normal part of life. Those of you reading this in your retirement will remember times when so many of the things that today we take for granted didn't exist. They hadn't been invented. Even younger people, and certainly those over thirty, will remember a time when computers, iPods and mobile phones did not play such a large part in everyone's lives. The incredible thing is that none of these things were really predicted fifty years ago which leads to the conclusion that the next fifty years are going to be just as unpredictable – at least by us. God of course knows exactly what's going to happen. Although the thought of a world managed according to God's principles might now seem just like an impossible dream, God has given human beings an amazing ability to create, invent, think and adapt. Change happens at an incredible pace in the modern world, and it can also happen unpredictably like changes in the natural systems we were thinking about earlier. Think of the collapse of communism. This was something that was almost completely unpredicted. God knew it was going to happen as he had planned it that way, but we didn't!

Living a simpler and slower lifestyle does not mean a return to the past. The previous industrial revolution brought so many benefits to society and we don't have to lose them. We don't have to return to the nineteenth century and send young boys up chimneys, but we will have to do things differently. We should be looking forward to the new Green Revolution that some people are already taking part in and make sure that Christians are playing a full and leading part so that this time God's principles of nature are at its heart.

And finally, if all this can be achieved, we should remember that it will still not be heaven on earth. Salvation is not going to be achieved through ecological sustainability! There will still be sin in the world and our Christian mission will be to bring people to Christ until he returns.

Further Reading

Thankfully, this is not the only book written on this topic! Here are some that I would recommend, each containing a longer list of publications if you want to follow through ideas in more detail.

A Christian Guide to Environmental Issues, Martin J Hodson and Margot R. Hodson (BRF 2015) – a useful book for a description of the ways in which we are damaging creation. The main focus is on a description of environmental issues from a Christian perspective, though there are theological insights as well.

Jesus and the Earth, by James Jones (SPCK 2003) – a really short book by James Jones, previously Bishop of Liverpool. This is an accessible read on the biblical mandate for creation care.

Planetwise - Dare to care for God's World, by Dave Bookless (IVP 2008) – a look at Christians and the environment from a theological perspective, but with practical suggestions as well.

L is for Lifestyle by Ruth Valerio (IVP 2008) – the second edition of a very practical book with lots of information about how Christians can live more creation care lives. Really useful if you are looking for practical ideas for action.

These books are also good but take a more scientific and theological approach:

When Enough is Enough – A Christian Framework for Environmental Sustainability edited by R.J Berry, (Apollos, 2007)

Christianity, Climate Change and Sustainable Living, Nick Spencer and Robert White (SPCK, 2007)

Christian web sites and organisations:

The John Ray Initiative (www.jri.org.uk) has a great website that you can trust. The best thing about the website is all the thoughtful papers you will find that look at a range of different aspects of creation care. You will find excellent papers by Professor Sam Berry if you don't have the time to read the whole book listed above!

The Christian Institute (www.christian.org.uk) is a well-known organisation and does a tremendous work speaking out on a range of social and moral issues. However, it is almost totally silent when it comes to creation care - which is puzzling.

A Rocha (www.arocha.org/gb-en/index.html) was founded in the UK in 1983 and is now the leading worldwide Christian environmental organisation with a large variety of practical and theological programmes for churches and individuals. A Rocha has five core commitments that were drafted by John Stott, a passionate supporter of the movement: Christian, Conservation, Community, Cross Cultural and Cooperation.

Operation Noah - www.operationnoah.org. On the Operation Noah website you will find a link from the home page to an excellent paper on climate change written by Professor Sir John Houghton, a Christian and an expert on climate change who was a member of the Inter-Governmental Panel on Climate Change (IPCC) and received the Nobel Prize. The Panel was awarded jointly with Al Gore. Be warned though. Although the rest of the Operation Noah site is interesting and has useful information and ideas, it takes a very broad approach to the Christian faith. As a result is a tricky site to feel comfortable with and read!

Green Christian (previously Christian Ecology Link, CEL) - www.greenchristian.org.uk. Green Christian was started in 1981 and is a very broadly based membership organisation that produces a regular magazine, organises a variety of events including an annual conference, and also has a number of on-going projects. GC produce a lot of good resources and the site has lots of news about Christian ecological events and news items giving a Christian perspective. A site well worth visiting - treading carefully at times!

Sources of Environmental Information:

There are literally hundreds of web sites with ecological information. The key thing is to use sites that have reliable and trustworthy data, interpreted in a fair way. The following sites I have used fit these criteria.

In general terms sites from the United Nations Environment Programme (www.unep.org), and the International Union for the Conservation of Nature (www.iucn.org) are good starting points and have summary articles about a range of ecological issues and links to other sources of reliable data. For the situation in the UK then the Defra website is as good as any (www.defra.gov.uk) and the information found on both the Friends of the Earth and WWF sites is also reliable (www.foe.co.uk and www.wwf.org.uk). The Living Planet Report from WWF is a great summary of the current ecological state of the planet.

There are also many specific subject websites. For climate change The Intergovernmental Panel on Climate Change (IPCC) has the latest reports. They are found on the publications pages and are called

"Assessment Reports". The summaries are the best documents to read (www.ipcc.ch) though still hard going. For economic issues the New Economics Foundation has some challenging thinking (www.neweconomics.org) which is well respected by governments and businesses. www.globalissues.org has some good issues pages, and www.developments.org.uk, from the Department for International Development also has some interesting information on the environmental and global issues.

Endnotes

[1] The best presentation of the SEI's Planetary Life Support Systems can be found in the New Scientist 27/2/2010

[2] The most detailed information about the Ecological Footprint can be found of the Global Footprint Network's website – www.footprintnetwork.org. The idea can get fairly complicated. One of the best calculators so that you can work out your own footprint is http://calculator.bioregional.com

[3] List of countries by ecological footprint. (2015, December 17). In *Wikipedia, The Free Encyclopedia*. Retrieved 18:00, January 1, 2016, from https://en.wikipedia.org/w/index.php?title=List_of_countries_by_ecological_footprint&oldid=695670258

[4] List of countries by ecological footprint. (2015, December 17). In *Wikipedia, The Free Encyclopedia*. Retrieved 18:00, January 1, 2016, from https://en.wikipedia.org/w/index.php?title=List_of_countries_by_ecological_footprint&oldid=695670258

[5] All the information about climate changes comes from the Intergovernmental Panel on Climate Change (IPCC). Go to their website - http://www.ipcc.ch - and download the *Summary for Policymakers for the latest Assessment Report* for more details.

[6] The term "affluenza" was made popular by Oliver James is his book of the same name.

[7] More information about the World Happiness Surveys can be found on the website http://www.worldvaluessurvey.org/

[8] I have used a variety of sources to get the data on making a T shirt. The simplest summary can be found on Youtube if you search for "The environmental impact of the cotton T-shirt".

[9] One example of the imbalance of consumption appears in the Times of India. http://timesofindia.indiatimes.com/india/US-eats-5-times-more-than-India-per-capita/articleshow/3008449.cms. The message that countries such as India hear is that the West wants them to reduce their populations so that we can carry on over-consuming!

[10] John Stott was one of the first evangelical leaders to speak out in "Issues Facing Christians Today" which is now in its fourth edition (Zondervan, 2006). It is a good read although the section on the environment is a little weak compared with some of the books in the Further Reading section.

[11] The United Nation website of their Department for Economic and Social Affairs (DESA) has a lot of robust statistical data on population growth. https://www.un.org/development/desa/en/

[12] http://www.lovefoodhatewaste.com/. This website is about the best for information about food waste. Statistics about the other information in this paragraph can be found by reading the latest WWF "Living Earth Report" published each year.

[13] There are few single sources of information about these issues. You will find up to date information by searching for "gold and environment" or "coltan" online. The listings of sites include news reports from the Guardian and BBC as well as the Society of Investigative Journalists.

[14] There are a growing number of books about poverty and wealth with the classic one being "Rich Christians in an Age of Hunger" by Ronald Sider (Thomas Nelson). Although some of the statistics are dated the theology is not!

[15] The Worldwide Fund for Nature (WWF) website has a lot of information about what people are doing to nearly every habitat and species. The UK and USA sites are both good. Just google "Environmental impact of..." and it will take you straight to the right page on the WWF sites.

[16] I must confess that I found all these quotes on www.goodreads.com!

[17] The best website in the UK for thinking about closed loop thinking or the circular economy (there are lots of different names from the same thing) is from the organisation founded by the round the world yachtswoman Dame Ellen Macarthur. http://www.ellenmacarthurfoundation.org/

[18] This whole section is about taking inspiration from how nature works to design the products we use today. As well as the "big picture" of closed loop thinking, designers are also using detailed ideas from nature in an approach called "biomimicry". Two web sites give lots of examples, www.biomimicry.org and www.asknature.com

[19] You can read about Ray Anderson on various environmental business websites, such as www.greenbiz.com/blog/2014/ 09/03/20-years-later-interface-looks-back-ray-andersons-legacy or you can read one of his books such as "Confessions of a Radical Industrialist: Profits, People, Purpose-Doing Business by Respecting the Earth".

[20] There are plenty of books around that show that God has provided enough of everything for everyone. The website of an organisation called Steady State is worth looking at, as is a book by Rob Dietz and Dan O'Neil called "Enough is Enough". The website is http://steadystate.org/

[21] The classic book on closed loop thinking that describes products like the chair is called "Cradle to Cradle" by Michael Braungart and William McDonough.

[22] This was famously said by Victor Lebow, Journal of Retailing, 1955, and is quoted in a wonderful cartoon presentation of over consumption called "The Story of Stuff". www.storyofstuff.org

[23] http://www.theconvergingworld.org/carbon_calculator. This site allows you to calculate the amount of CO_2 generated by almost any journey you might want to make.